I have a story for you ...

by:

Carole Bertuzzi Luciani

This book was written, edited and self-published by the author; with Library and Archives Canada registration, cover layout and styling, and production management through the TRI Publishing division of TRIMATRIX Management Consulting Inc.
www.trimatrixmanagement.com

For information, please contact: cbluc@cogeco.ca

First edition.
Published and printed in Canada

Library and Archives Canada Cataloguing in Publication

Bertuzzi Luciani, Carole, 1952-
     I have a story for you-- / Carole Bertuzzi Luciani.

ISBN 978-1-897412-83-1

     1. Life--Anecdotes. I. Title.

PN6261.B46 2009   C818'.602   C2009-904150-2

TRI Publishing is a division
of T R I M A T R I X
Management Consulting Inc.
www.trimatrixconsulting.ca

Setting the Tone

I have a story for you ... and if I had the chance, I'd tell it to you rather than have you read it. But that's because I'm a talker, not a writer. As a matter of fact, if my second year English prof knew about this book he'd shake his head in disbelief. He issued me an embarrasing F + as a final mark for his course, The Use and The Abuse of the English Language. When I signed up for the course I figured that based on the title my chances of getting a 50 were pretty well wrapped up. But despite my pleadings he refused to budge in his assessment of my talent, believing that a 49.5 was the only way I'd get the message. Undeterred by my failure I bravely enrolled in Creative Writing the following semester. My prof Edie, deemed my work worthy of an A-, thereby restoring my confidence and enthusiasm.

Fast forward to now, and I believe I have settled somewhere in the middle of the two streams of teaching. And, thanks to the help of my longstanding friend and grammar critic Paula, I am not ashamed of the writing that follows.

I am not a Celebrity. Well, maybe a small 'c' celebrity because I have appeared in the local paper numerous times, albeit usually in a clown's outfit and wearing a red nose, but I do have the print as evidence.

I have also appeared on a number of international T.V.

shows like *Oprah, Donahue, Geraldo, The Jenny Jones Show, Regis* and *The Dini Petty Show* ... but only in the audience. Still, that's got to count for something.

Maybe you have seen me on the local cable channel. Well, maybe not ... we all know how many viewers that draws.

Add to this impressive list of credentials that I am a highly 'ah claimed' moodivational speaker. My father once reported to my brother, Larry, after hearing me speak for the first and only time, "Ah, she wasn't too bad." If you knew my father, you'd know that's quite a compliment.

The one thing I have done to earn the write ... oops, I mean the right to publish this book is that I have LIVED for over fifty-seven years, all of the time watching, listening and participating in life as it swirls around me. My father used to incessantly nag us with: "If you just stop and pay attention, damn it, you just might learn something."

So learn I did and continue to do. I've learned that stuff happens and it's how you react to it that's important. And I've learned that funny is everywhere. If you look for it, you'll be sure to find it. It presents itself in a multitude of forms and situations. The key is to stop and recognize it for what it is.

I hope that when you read my stories you will see that this approach to life helps to both ease the pain it sometimes presents and share its many pleasures. Perhaps they will encourage you to be more receptive to the humour that crosses your own path. Then when we meet, you might say to me, "I have a story for YOU ..."

Enjoy ~!!~

A special Thank You to ...

My family, Joe, Dante, Vince and Alena for providing both the stress and the humour in my life. May the mention of your name in these stories remind you of the special role you continue to play.

My friends who are the characters in some of the stories. I will not single anyone out. You know who you are. You make me laugh out loud; you laugh with me when we're together; and you bring out the 'funny' in me. And for that I am grateful.

Paula McParland Hall, my friend since grade five, who forever has been my pocket grammar guide. I know I am a better speaker and now a writer because of your corrections along the way. Can we ever forget my question to you from grade nine, "Who wrote this book 'Ibid' anyway? Everyone seems to have read it but me." I could not have imagined doing this with anyone else.

Linda Jodoin Emberley ... my techno-whiz friend responsible for the layout of the book and the photos. Linda tries hard not to remind me what a techno-phobe I really am. Thanks for biting your tongue and biding your time throughout the whole ordeal. And please promise me you will not share those rejected photos with anyone.

My 'readers', Joe, Natalie, Kathy, Maryann, Lisa, Marjory, Liz, Julie and Anne ... without your initial 'reading and ranking', I would never have known that someone other than myself might enjoy these. Your input was invaluable.

Chris Desforges ... for your creative touches to the cover. You were adept at combining my whims with your ways.

Sheryl Lubbock ... for guiding me through the self-publishing process. I am so happy we had that initial meeting through the Company of Women.

Finally, to every audience I have had the pleasure to speak to ... for giving me your time and attention and listening to my stories.

Your Reading List

Dedication

The following stories are dedicated to the three people who have made the most significant impact on my life ... my grandmother Nona, my father Peo and my husband Joe. Together, you have made me laugh, kept me honest and let me be me. I'll let you figure out who is responsible for what.

Nona's Unstressing

I learned many valuable lessons from my grandmother. As a child, I idolized her, so of course I paid very close attention to everything she said and all that she did.

We called her Nona. Her name was Brandina Vallesi Ferroni Silenzi. She was a woman who never had the opportunity to learn to read or write. She came over from Italy at seven, and went to school for only a few months before going to work in the cotton mill. However, this did not prevent her from evolving into a very wise woman.

Although she signed everything with an 'X', she knew exactly the terms and conditions presented on each page of every document. She subscribed to daily delivery of The Hamilton Spectator so she could keep up with current events by looking at the pictures. And she rarely missed a news broadcast or a talk show. Nona had warmth, Nona had wit and Nona had wisdom and she shared these qualities with us every chance she got. When she did, I was always there to embrace them with open arms.

Nona used to come from Hamilton to visit us in Thorold. When we were told Nona was coming for a few days it was a definite cause for celebration, not only because of the wonderful meals we would be enjoying, but also because we loved having her around to tell us stories and make us laugh.

We would wait excitedly on the street for her arrival (Nona

loved royal welcomes). One of our relatives would deliver her, and she would always arrive carrying only one small suitcase and one large glass jug of fresh Hamilton water. Nona believed that the paper mill in Thorold had a greater contamination effect on our water than the steel plants of Hamilton had on theirs.

The first thing we would do after wrapping our short arms around her large middle was take her suitcase. We would then run off and hide it. We did that because we thought that if Nona couldn't find her suitcase she'd never leave.

Nona's visits meant that Sharon and I would share our room with her. We had two single beds, but gladly slept like spoons in one of them so that Nona could have the other one to herself ... at least until morning, when we would climb into bed with her to enjoy her warmth.

Each night we would coerce Nona into coming to bed early so that she could be with us until we fell asleep. Well, getting Nona to bed was no easy task. She had her routines. She would spend time in the bathroom preparing ... taking her milk of magnesia pills, liver pills, iron pills, as well as pills for her heart, arthritis and any other ailment she had at the time. While all of this was taking place, Sharon and I would repeatedly call out, "C'mon Nona, hurry up!" But Nona didn't hurry up for anybody.

She carried about two hundred and forty-five pounds (I have a lot to look forward to) and had 'bad legs'. When she moved, she did it with a sway and a waddle that only a frame carrying a lot of weight can do. Her response to our pleas to hurry were always the same: she'd wave her hand up by the side of her head like she was giving the royal acknowledgement and shake her head gently from side to side, advising us, "Ah, figlia ('loved one' in Italian) ... I'ma not ready yet!"

My nona would then waddle on over to the edge of the bed as she complained about how hard it was for an old lady to get down so low. Although the laws of etiquette at the time dictated that ladies sit with their legs together, trying to keep them parallel while attempting to sit down is a next-to-impossible task when you're dealing with an abundance of flesh. When Nona lowered her bum to a seat, you could hear the gentle swoosh as her flesh spread out, giving her great comfort. All of this maneuvering was accompanied by a satisfied grunt.

We would continue to urge her to hurry, unable to understand what could possibly take her so long, and again she'd cock that hand and inform us that she was not yet ready. After all, she was still in her house dress. So, with me peering from behind Sharon, we would wait and watch, not wanting to miss anything.

Nona changed into her flannelette nightgown with the knack and know-how of someone who had done this thousands of times. At the time, we didn't realize that the image of this procedure would remain with us for the rest of our lives, and that we would even employ it once or twice ourselves when modesty dictated. What we witnessed was magic, because although men may fantasize about watching a woman undress, little do they know that we are all armed with the skills and talent to get ourselves out of any piece of clothing and into our flannelettes without exposing one inch of skin.

Nona cleverly unbuttoned her dress, wriggled her arms out, then lowered it to her feet as she simultaneously dropped the flannelette over her head. We then enjoyed the benefit of the sound effects as she wiggled out of her corset. You know those beigey/pinky/salmony coloured garments that came in one big piece and were meant to encase an oversized body, change its shape and torture the wearer at the same time?

First, we'd hear the ch-ch-ch-ch-ch-ch-ch-ch of the twenty-four sets of hooks and eyes, then we'd hear the zzzip-zzzip of the two zippers. The finale came when we'd hear the ftt-ftt, ftt-ftt, ftt-ftt of the laces which signified the blessed release of Nona's body on the bed. Incredulous, my sister and I had no idea that one day we, too, would experience the mystique of corset-like clothing, albeit in a less medieval form.

"C'mon, Nona, hurry up. You're taking so long!"

And again, she'd reply, "Figlia, I'm a not ready yet."

Nona still had more to her routine. Placing her hands on both knees, she took a deep breath and with her lips still fixed loosely together, she rolled out every ounce of old breath from her body. Her cheeks would tremble as the sound ricocheted between her lips making a distinctive outboard motor-like sound. Of course, we'd laugh at her antics, and through our giggles we'd squeal, "Nona, why do you do that?"

With the cock of her hand again she'd say, "Ah, figlia. It makesa me feel good. You standa around all day, you cooka, you cleana, you listena to people's problems, you take it inna. If you take it inna and you dona let it go, it comes out in other places."

What Nona was advocating back then is actually one of the most useful and effective stress management techniques we know. When you feel the tension, you've got to breathe deep and let it go. Occasionally, I even indulge in a good old fashioned Nona-style motorized sigh to go along with it. And to steal her words, ah, it makesa me feel so good!

He Always Kept His Promise

*G*rowing up in the fifties, we were influenced by the shows we saw on our new black and white TV sets. It seemed we were particularly drawn to and intrigued by the shows that depicted families. There were so many back then, each with a mother who stayed home and a dad who went to work. In each episode, some interesting situation occurred and was quickly resolved before the half hour was up. And it seemed that it was the father in the family who was generally in charge.

Episodes often included a coming-home-from-work scene. In one of my favourite shows, *Father Knows Best*, the dad would pull into the driveway after a day at work. On cue, regardless of where the children were playing or how deeply involved in fun they might be, everything would be dropped so that they could scamper off to welcome him home. They would huddle around him, hugging his leg and gripping his arm; one would take his briefcase and together they would saunter towards the front door.

There stood his adoring wife, dressed in her wool skirt and sweater set, wearing a freshly starched apron. As he stepped onto the porch, she would extend her arms and welcome him home. The kids would dash off to clean up before dinner and soon they'd all be sitting around the dining room table. There the dinner would be served: a pot roast, mashed potatoes and vegetables. There would be no fighting, no burping, no yelling and certainly no passing of gas. When dinner ended, they would all thank their mother, hug their father and run off to get ready for bed.

Funny, but somehow that did not depict our family. In our home, whenever any of us (usually me) had caused or gotten into some trouble that day, my mother would wag her finger in our direction voicing the threat, "You wait until your father gets home." Consequently, no matter where we were or what we were doing when we saw our dad's Pontiac drive along Whyte Avenue, all was dropped and we'd charge in the opposite direction.

My dad was a good man; he was hardworking, honest and exceptionally conscientious about his role as father. Those were also the traits that made us so afraid of him. He didn't believe in providing bumper pads for us in life and was determined to keep us on the straight and very narrow path. Consequences were to be paid for any deviation from that path and in the spirit of consistency, he followed through with every single threat. This tough approach to discipline was a result of his having to parent his six younger siblings after the premature death of their father when my dad was nine.

The year that Sharon and I did well enough in school to earn our new bikes was a momentous one for us. It meant liberation from ever having to ride 'double' again and the freedom to ride to the other side of Thorold. Oh, how we loved those bikes. Since we shared everything else, having our very own bikes meant that they became our most prized possessions. We each saved our money to adorn the CCMs with bike gear such as mudguards, streamers and mirrors. We excitedly entered bicycle rodeos to show off our souped-up bikes and riding skills.

In between riding adventures, we'd often stop off at home to regroup before heading out again. When we did, we'd basically roll into the driveway and jump off, dropping the bike with the back wheels still spinning. It was common to see the Bertuzzi driveway littered with bikes.

One night when our dad returned home from work, he couldn't get into the driveway because of such a scene. He knew right away that our CCMs were involved. A bunch of us were playing in the backyard. Without hesitation, he came storming back, his face screwed up with fury. Centering Sharon and I out, he yelled, "The next time I come home from work and I see your bikes in the driveway, I'm gonna drive right over them." Knowing he'd be true to his word the two of us vowed to obey.

Same scene a few nights later, except that this time our bikes were parked up against the house. Playing out back with our friends, we suddenly heard a crunching sound come from the driveway. We ran out to see what it was. Our dad had kept his promise, driving right over the bike that had been left lying on the driveway. Except it wasn't ours. It belonged to our friend Juliana and he quickly knew it by the expressions on all of our faces. We dared not say one word and quietly led the stricken Juliana back into the yard.

The last picture I have is of Dad in the garage with the bike in a vice, muttering to himself.

He actually did a nice job straightening the wheel and putting it back together. Although things hadn't exactly gone the way he intended, he had definitely made his point. It wasn't necessary to publish a notice in the weekly church bulletin citing the rule of the Bertuzzi driveway; after that day, all of our friends knew it.

The Black Dress

My mother used to sew all of my dresses. I use the word 'all' lightly, because a dress rarely found its way onto my back more than once or twice a year. One year she made me a black dress in a slinky polyester fabric. It hugged my body nicely and had a cowl neckline that draped in folds across my chest. Simple, yet tasteful, just the way I liked it (and still do).

The black dress was Joe's favourite. He said I looked sexy in it, and that he loved the way it felt when we danced. So I wore it a lot during our first few years together. Then it inevitably met its fate at the hands of a household policy developed to avoid overly cluttered closets: 'What comes in goes out'. This meant that whenever I got a new dress I had to get rid of an older one. It was time to say bye-bye to the black dress, so off it went to be recycled at the Nearly New Shop run by the Hospital Auxiliary.

The winter after I donated it, Joe asked what had happened to the black dress. He was upset that of all the junk (his words) I had, I chose to get rid of *that* dress. I told him my decision had to do with a stage I was going through. I was trying to cut my emotional ties with the colour black, after suffering years of addiction to it. Nose out of joint for an extended time, he never missed an opportunity to mutter, "Your black dress would have been perfect to wear tonight," whenever he could get away with it.

Eventually, though, he had to join me in letting it go.

The next spring, the Auxiliary decided to host a fashion show to promote their selection of nearly new clothing. They asked me to be the commentator and I accepted, knowing I could have a lot of fun with it. A week before the show, a meeting was arranged for the committee to review the clothes that had been picked to be in it. We rummaged through the racks together, and I diligently made notes about each piece to help with my commentary. Trying to be helpful, the ladies contributed their own comments about each garment. As we made our way toward the end of the selection, one of the women announced, "Oh, yes, and there's this thing here. I have no idea what you can say about it ... who on earth would wear it?

Tch, tch-ing" and nodding their heads in unison, they all agreed that it was hideous.

I looked at the limp piece of black polyester hanging for all its life on an old wire hanger and felt that there was something vaguely familiar about it. Then it hit me (you know where this is going). I yelled, "Hey! That's my dress. Give me that."

They looked at me, assuming I was joking. I am sure they were collectively thinking she wouldn't possibly wear that thing ... would she? You better believe it! I yanked my black dress off the hanger and slung it proudly over my shoulder. If they thought I should be embarrassed ... they were wrong.

The show was a great success and my preparation had paid off. The commentary went over well and I was a hit. Of course, I wore my black dress and accessorized it beautifully with a black hat and gloves. People couldn't believe that I had dressed myself from the Nearly New Shop, especially the flabbergasted ladies from the Auxiliary.

Although this was all very satisfying, the best part was Joe's reaction when he saw me in the dress that night. He was very very happy. And he was right; the dress was perfect.

Big Time Baseball

I have been playing baseball since I was a first grader in Thorold, Ontario. Every recess we would claim the upper left-hand paved corner of the playground and set up our teams. Since we were in the middle of the dominant Yankee years I was called Mickalina Mantle, a name to which I answered with great pride.

My playground accomplishments earned me early entry into the local 'Bird League'. Since I was two years younger than the rest of the players (albeit four inches taller), I was assigned the unenviable position of back catcher. Not only was this a dangerous spot to be, but my extra height behind the shorter batters made it an uncomfortably low crouch. When I was twelve I was allowed to play in two all-boys Little League hardball games. My career with them ended abruptly when someone complained. So was I too good or what?

When I wasn't playing, I was watching. I loved the sound of the ball hitting the catcher's mitt and especially liked the look of the old style uniforms. And how I wished I had a pair of those flat-soled sneakers like the boys. They left such a great imprint in the dirt.

My playing days continued until the end of high school. I loved baseball. Each year Joe and I enjoyed a game with our friends. Supposedly a fun game, few of those annual fests ever ended in harmony. Many a relationship became strained from those pick-up games. My own was most affected the year Joe was the ump and we lost the game on a call he barely saw!!!!!!!

The summer after Dante was born I decided to recapture my passion for the game. It had been at least fifteen years since I had played in an organized, no fighting-cheating-or swearing format. I flipped through the local Parks and Recreation booklet in search of information about the league I had seen playing the previous summer. I had watched them with envy, knowing I could play with the best of them. It made me realize how much I missed the game. Ah, there it was. The ad read: 'Oakville Ladies Recreational Softball League, a fun and recreational program for women of all ages. No experience necessary'. It was a perfect fit for my needs.

I registered and was assigned to a team. Within days, a call came from the coach, inviting me to the first practice. I was excited. I dug out my old glove, the one I got when I was six from an uncle who lived in New York. I had banked on it being blessed by the Yankees themselves and it had served me well for all those years. To restore its life I massaged it well with linseed oil, tucked a ball in the pocket and kept it tied until the day of the practice. I loved the way it felt, the sound it made when I flapped the padded fingers together (a habit I still have as I wait for the throw to first). And it made me smile to see the dotted C.B. that I had burned into the leather with a magnifying glass in the sunshine of a long ago day as I stood out in lonely right field. It didn't concern me that my hand had grown to such a length that the glove grooves were now only slightly longer than my own fingers. When I put on that glove it felt wonderful!

Next, I had to find a pair of shoes. Other than a worn pair of tennis shoes, all I had was a pair of funky orange canvas ones whose claim to fame was that the same style had once been in a Pizza Pizza commercial. They would be perfect. Before I left I decided I needed a prop, so I grabbed my slide whistle, figuring it would come in handy for acknowledging good plays.

A little nervous and still carrying a few extra pounds from the first pregnancy, I arrived at the park. Oooh! I even remember the smell of freshly cut grass. I loved the way the loose dust of the infield billowed around my every imprint and how my socks took on that clay coloured tone. Oh, and that smacking sound you can hear whenever ball makes contact with glove. A few practice throws and I recognized the effects of aging on my arm. I used to be the 'ball throw' queen at the annual school track meets. That ball used to sail. I could easily throw a strike from centre to home without a strain. But now, with the elasticity no longer what it once was, perhaps first base was meant to be my new home.

Soon, our two coaches lassoed us in for a meeting. Nice guys, the kind who wore their day jobs with pride under their fingernails. They were a little gruff but hey, they were good enough to volunteer their time to be with us women. They deserved credit for that.

Checking out my teammates, I noticed that some were quite friendly ... with one another. They obviously had played together before. A few looked scared as they put the death grip to their stiff new gloves, and others were oblivious to the fact that they threw 'just like a girl' (which stands as the greatest insult to a ball player). One woman who was a smoker had the idea that a good warm-up meant reaching for her lighter. Some of the players took this ball business so seriously they tugged on body parts they didn't have, mimicking the big leaguers. They strutted, knees flipping to the outside with every stride. I swear I even saw one spit, a skill I didn't realize girls had. What an eclectic crew we were!

Looking around, I realized that we truly represented a wide variety of females. In my mind, I fast forwarded to the time when we would gel as a team. This was a component that fascinated me. Typically, with a baseball team, it happens after the first night in the pub. I was looking forward to the process.

Time to listen up, the coaches had us where they wanted us ... down on the grass so they could loom large over us. A few organizational bits of information were shared, and then one took charge. He bellowed: "Before we begin, there's somethin' we have to discuss as a team so us coaches know what to expect from you. Do ya wanna win? Or do ya just wanna have fun?"

Oooh! What a dilemma! I thought the two were an automatic couple. I didn't do anything in my life without an element of fun. Why bother if it's not going to be fun? I gathered the courage to speak in front of all these strangers (a risk I take regularly now).

Hand waving in the air, I started: "Ah, excuse me, but as one of those obnoxious Type A overachievers (I had just recently managed to reverse my longstanding underachiever status), I was kinda hoping that we could win and have fun while we do it!"

Heads bobbed in agreement like the puppy dogs in the back of cars, but the coach barked back with: "It can't be done!"

Right then I knew it would be a rocky season. My slide whistle even seemed to bristle in my sweatpants pocket, but I was determined to see my plan through.

The team uniforms were distributed. My goodness, how depressing. Imagine trying to play a competitive game of ball wearing beige jerseys. We blended with the infield. We pouted. There is no subliminal power source to beige. We spent the next half hour trying to figure out how we could give life to these sad shirts, short of spray-painting them. I embraced the challenge and painted socks for many of us on the team. If nothing else, they diverted attention away from our tops.

Each game we got better. We were coming together as a team and I knew my teammates appreciated my lighthearted approach to the game. I whistled after every good play. We hooted. We hollered and we hugged a whole bunch. But the other teams were so serious. They sneered and snarled at my wisecracks from first base. They cringed at the sound of the shrilling whistle. They rolled their eyes at our pregame chants (the leadership of which I had accepted with pleasure). They gripped the wire fence and vented their opinions about every play. During one game, the coach from the other team was so angry that after going chest to chest with the umpire to no avail, he picked up all the bats and flung them onto the infield. Standing frozen in the infield, I tried to recall whether I had received my pay cheque for this yet.

So much for 'fun and recreational'.

The more I witnessed this behaviour the more I was determined to have some fun. Every at-bat, I'd take my time wiggling into position. I'd motion to the fielders to back it up. To this day I'm certain I still hold the record for the longest single in the league. I'd yell out to them: "Pack a lunch!"

Getting set at the plate, I'd envision this same scene in my second favourite movie, *The Natural*. (*A League of Their Own*, in number one spot, still makes me cry). I'd imagine hitting the cover off the ball and fireworks erupting everywhere. I always finished my routine with a smile to the pitcher, pointing to where I wanted her to pitch the ball.

One night the tension was as thick as the dust at our feet. It was a close game and we desperately wanted to beat this team. It was my turn at bat. I swung my hips into position, set the mental images in gear and was ready. Just as the umpire leaned forward to motion for the pitch, I heard yelling from the coach of the opposing team. Hands cupped to his mouth, he screamed, "She's big, but she's easy!"

Well. I couldn't believe what I was hearing. I have tolerated my share of verbal torment and teasing over the years but I was not going to tolerate this. I straightened up, dropped the bat, extended my index finger and went at him. "Hey buddy. I don't take that kinda talk from my own husband. I'm sure as hell not going to take it from you!"

The women cheered. The umpire whipped off his mask and stepped to the plate. With his hands in the 'T' position, he roared, "Time called!" Pointing to the coach he bellowed,

"You! Keep your mouth shut and that's a warning! And you, (his spit now sprinkling my face) get up to bat. We're playing a serious game here!"

I got a hit that at-bat. Although we lost the game, we headed to the pub with plenty to talk about. That night, we came together as a team. We pledged to put 'fun and recreational' into every game.

I zealously pursued this mission until my retirement from baseball in 2000.

The Rexall Revues

As soon as I entered the grey, dimly lit concrete factory of Rexall Drug Company I knew I was about to get a taste of another world. This was not something I looked forward to. At seventeen, the life I lived was pretty sheltered and I had no idea what to expect from a job in a factory. On my first day, I dragged myself in for a 7:00 a.m. start. I was directed to work on the busy aerosol line. It was popular because a lot of piece-work could be earned, and on Saturdays, you earned time and a half. That was a lot of money for a high school student, so I knew that no matter how bad it was, I would stick it out.

During that first shift I was introduced to people I would not ordinarily meet up with in my teenage travels. Some were single moms, some carried bruises on their bodies like badges, some spoke no English and a few had no teeth. Some women worked to pay for their new refrigerator or stove while others had to pay the rent. A very few were there to fulfill their dreams of having expensive possessions.

I was open to meeting these new people. I enjoyed watching them and listening to their colourful language, and I even managed to pick up a few choice words that had to be systematically stricken from my vocabulary before returning to school in the fall. Being among this crowd was an adventure in its own way (case in point: on the very first day I witnessed a fistfight between two smocked women on the assembly line) and I told myself that all I had to do was find a way to survive those two short months. I could fight it or I could join in. I decided to join.

The only problem was that I hated the work. To help pass the boredom of the menial tasks I was expected to perform, I spent my time talking to Bob, whose only job was to deliver boxes to us. I'd work like a madwoman as he stood beside me chatting me up.

Every fifteen minutes I would yell, "boxes!" or "palett!" loud enough to remind him that he was supposed to be working too.

My co-workers teased me about this relationship; they called me 'school girl' and took pride in advising me on the ways of the floor. They wanted to be as much a part of my world as I would allow. If I learned anything that summer, it was that I'd better stay in school; piecework or no piecework, I definitely didn't want to be on the assembly line forever.

By summer's end, I was relieved to say goodbye to factory life. No more grey concrete surroundings, no more punching in and out, and thankfully, no more mindless activities governed by the sound of the buzzer. It seemed like I had spent my whole summer waiting for the clock to signal a break or time to go home.

The next spring they invited me back to work again. I would not have been interested, but they had decided to create a student shift from 4:00-11:00 p.m. This had enormous appeal. I immediately solicited a few of my best friends to join me. I was sure it was going to be a different experience altogether. It was gonna be fun.

That summer we had a supervisor named Mike. He discussed his mandate at the first meeting. There were quotas to be reached. He was determined to show administration that a late shift of young people could keep production lines going and maintain volume according to the standards of workmanship and safety that had been set. Besides, the idea of having his daytime hours free appealed to him. Administration was not convinced that it was a good idea, but had agreed to try it.

Every day just before 4:00, we would dash through the doors of the factory in a panic to punch in on time. No one liked to be docked fifteen minutes of pay for being two minutes late. As we entered, my friends from the year before were leaving from their day shift. There were catcalls and whistles from the men in blue, and the women loved to yell out, "Hey school girl, how ya doin'?"

This recognition was always a comforting beginning to my shift. They would often stare at us and wonder why we appeared to be so eager to get out on the floor. They certainly couldn't have recalled me being so enthusiastic the previous summer. Unbelievably, we didn't want to miss a minute.

You see it wasn't long before our gang of fifteen became friends. Standing at our designated posts in smocks and hairnets, we wasted no time getting to know one another. We managed to keep our chins wagging most of the shift. The girls all worked the lines and the machines while our male counterparts earned forty percent more, doing nothing more than keeping us supplied with boxes and palettes ... an injustice that did not go unnoticed.

The guys passed their time by checking in at each post regularly throughout each shift. By enjoying regular and alternating visits with each of us, they were better equipped to make our social plans for the next day. Most of us spent our days together playing golf, tennis or just hanging out. Friendships developed and relationships blossomed. It was like summer camp in the factory. Most nights after punching out, we would head to the local pub until closing. We seemed to fit the work in around all of our other activities.

Before too long it was obvious that Mike was pleased with our production. Initially he gave us opportunities to try out various jobs within the plant, but it soon became clear that we had each established our specialties. Some mastered the label machine, one made great corrugated boxes, two did wonders on the pill line, three controlled the shampoo line, two gently handled the toothpaste and a few of us were the whiz kids of the petroleum line.

Every night our conversations got more interesting, breaks were longer and our energy levels reached new heights. We motivated each other to reach the production maximum, earning us large rewards for piecework. Our daily activities fuelled us for an evening of stimulating conversation, uncontrollable laughter and unruly behaviour.

By our third week, we started holding impromptu skits on Friday night. Before the end of the summer, this became a weekly activity. Lines shut down at 9:30 p.m. for some serious fun. Performances were applauded while the doughnuts and pop were devoured. Knowing we could earn this time off ensured that the shampoo bottles kept getting filled, aerosol cans labeled, pills packaged and cartons of Vaseline jars sent off in record time.

By mid summer, the reports showed that our productivity had exceeded the day shift's numbers. Soon, new product lines were opened and new tasks presented. The reports from administration were full of accolades for the students. I'm certain that they scratched their heads in wonder over what the magic formula was for our success.

We had figured out that our bizarre factory behaviour could continue as long as our goals were met. No one ever knew about our non-stop chatter, impromptu camp song concerts or skits in the side room. We never shared our tricks with anyone or left behind the remnants of the night before. The numbers recorded at the end of our shift spoke for themselves.

That summer the fifteen of us enjoyed our jobs in the factory. In fact, many in the group would still likely say that it was their favourite summer job experience. The reason is simple. We liked one another (in fact, two of them got married). We respected each other. We got along and enjoyed each other's company. Most importantly, we had fun together.

No wonder we exceeded their expectations.

Bingo's in My Blood

If we had a family emblem, a Bingo card would probably be on it. In one way or another, this game of chance has always been a part of my life. My earliest encounter with the familiar numbered card was in our parish hall in Thorold where the moms would gather to play (apparently it falls short of the standards for gambling and is therefore okay). We little kids would try to sit quietly and watch as we tore up perforated red squares to be used as the markers. We dared not fidget or sneeze for fear of blowing them off our moms' cards. The rule was clear: no talking or carrying on at Bingo.

As I got a little older, I realized the hold that the game had on my own mother. A typical scene would go like this: After dinner my mother would announce in an exhausted state, "Oh, I feel all in. I think after dinner I'll just go to bed."

Then, while we were clearing the table the phone would ring. Inevitably, it was her 'Bingo buddy' calling. We'd listen carefully to catch the hushed conversation.

"You wanna go? I just have to make him his coffee and I can be ready."

Within minutes, my mom would be reaching for her crocheted pouch that contained markers, trinkets and tape and out the door she'd fly. We wouldn't know if she'd had a successful night until morning, when we'd roll over in bed to see if there was a little bit of cash on the night table. She always shared her winnings.

My mom endured a lot of teasing about her leisure pursuit and I will not dwell on the frequency or costs involved. All we knew was that Bingo was something she enjoyed and since she wasn't going into debt or committing a crime we should all just back off. And we did.

As I got older and embraced a frenetic pace of life, my mom would often comment, "You have to relax. At the rate you're going, you're not going to last. You should play Bingo. It really relaxes me."

Surely, she was joking. I couldn't think of anything I would rather not do to relax. For me, relaxing had to involve movement, music or at least indulging in something mood altering, like beer. But one night, my friend (and daughter of the Bingo buddy) and I decided to join our moms for a night out lookin' under the B.

What started with the phone call was followed by the retrieval of the pouch and the snatch of the sweater. My mom only wore one sweater to Bingo because of the smell it absorbed from the smokers in the room, a smell she never seemed to notice, despite being a non-smoker.

The first thing I noted as we headed out the front door was the spring in my mom's step. It was as if a weight had been lifted and a new spirit was unveiled. All the way there, my friend and I sat in the back seat, keeping our comments to ourselves as we listened to the excited chatter about the night's outing between the two women up front. It was certainly a far cry from our own outings, which typically involved hitting a bar.

Arriving at the hall (location varied depending on the night of the week and what specials were being offered), the car would barely be put in park before the doors would fly open, pouches flung and arms pumped to propel the ladies towards that counter. Ah yes, the counter that presented the menus for the night ... the Bingo cards. Guarding them with the fervor of secret agents were the service club volunteers, most of whom were unprepared for what the night would bring in the way of abuse.

As we approached the counter we saw many people who appeared to be just as excited as our moms. Was I missing something here? Because one thing I definitely wasn't feeling was excitement. If anything, I was getting nervous. These people had a look in their eyes that seemed to scream: Get outa my way, I need my cards!

They arrived with canes, oxygen tanks, work uniforms, housecoats, kids in tow. Some were alone, firmly clutching their handbags. From each one I heard what sounded like very complicated systems for purchasing their cards.

"I want ten cards: two from the top, three from the bottom, five randomly picked from the middle. At least two must have the number seven in the top right corner and don't you dare smudge a number with your finger."

As I watched my mom make her purchase, I saw that something had happened to her. Before my eyes, she had transformed into a woman on a mission. She had the determined look that was usually reserved for entering a fabric store (she was a skilled and passionate seamstress). Completing our purchase, she handed me my cards, all ten of them, including the 'specials'. Fingering what seemed like a thick bundle, my anxiety increased. As a never-was-but-should've-been diagnosed person with A.D.D. I knew I was in trouble. I couldn't possibly follow all of these numbers. Why did I get myself into this?

With the daughters trailing, the moms dashed to a section of the room which clearly belonged to them. The territory had been staked and everyone knew that this was where they sat. We claimed our spots, pulled out the extra chairs to make more elbowroom for scanning the cards, then got down to the preparatory ritual. Cards were laid out side by side and taped to secure them in place. Pouches sat open in front holding the coloured plastic discs; good luck trinkets were placed where they could be easily seen; lottery tickets were bought; Cokes were snapped opened. Each of us took a deep breath to get ready to play the first game.

With the caller's opening words, I heard a nearby groan and

irritated complaint. "Not this guy again. He mumbles. I can't hear a word he says."

Clearly, others felt the same way because a few yelled out, "Speak up! How the hell do you expect us to hear you?"

My friend and I stared at each other, afraid to utter a peep. At one point, we laughed at an outburst coming from someone nearby and got *the look* from an ardent player at the next table. Her piercing eyes might as well have bellowed, "Shut the hell up and just keep your eyes down!"

As I fumbled with my markers trying to keep up, my mom's hands danced over her cards accounting for every called number. When she finished checking her own cards, she'd glance over at mine, marking various spots and proclaiming, "You missed one."

The more numbers I covered and the closer I got to achieving the desired 'one line, two lines, T, X or L', the more nervous I got. Just when the heart palpitations were starting to kick in, my mom smiled at me and said, "Isn't this relaxing?"

NOOOOOOOO, I think I'm having a heart attack. The smoke filled room didn't help things either. How they managed to drink, smoke and play their cards I'll never know. I could barely concentrate on placing a marker on the appropriate numbers. The only tension-breaking bit of levity came from watching and listening to the antics of the other Bingo players as they tried to assert their control. If they heard a number called too often they'd yell at the caller, "Shake up your balls, buddy!"

When he announced "O-66," in unison they'd reply, "clickety click!"

And, at the sound of "B-4," the roar of "and after!" would be deafening.

There was a cadence and rhythm to the game and although talking was absolutely taboo, barking back to the caller was fair game.

None of us won that night. If we had, the money would have been split amongst us, and probably even shared with someone at home. All the way home, the conversation resembled that of a played euchre hand or the just completed round of golf. It went something like this:

"Well, when I got down to two numbers for that full card I had already paid off my Sears account in my head."

"That darn N-35 didn't get called all night."

"If I heard I-19 one more time I was going to run up and snatch it from the cage."

My friend and I never forgot our first real adult taste of B-I-N-G-O. Whenever we saw each other in the years that followed, we'd laugh and remember that first outing with our moms.

They have each long since retired from the game. However, I know my mom's pouch remains in the cupboard above the phone and I'm certain her Bingo sweater can still be found in the back corner of the hall closet. I even bet that if one night I suggested an outing to Bingo, my mom's eighty-nine year old legs would jump at the chance to go.

Pass the Pasta

I met Joe in January, 1976. It was actually a re-introduction because we had met each other for the first time ten years earlier. The attraction was instant. We became friendly immediately and it wasn't long before Joe announced to his parents that we were dating. This pleased them since they had heard about me from family friends. They knew of the Bertuzzi family (it's a small world in the Hamilton Italian community) and were acquainted with some of my relatives. They were happy for Joe. I must be a good girl.

They wanted to meet me, so before long I got the big invitation. Would I come over for Sunday lunch? No big deal. I'm used to these Italian family gatherings and besides, Joe's an only child, which eliminates a lot of distraction. I arrived on time, cleaned and polished, with gift neatly tucked in hand. I was confident of having made 'la bella figura', the all-important first impression.

I watched as Joe hugged both of his parents, planting warm kisses on each side of their faces. I smiled in the background. Then, in Italian, Joe proudly introduced me. His mother, a tiny woman, reached up with both hands, grabbed my face and pulling it down to her level and smacked me with kisses on both cheeks. His father smiled, put his hands on my shoulders and repeated the pattern. I felt that I had been very well welcomed even though I had no clue what they were saying to me.

For all I knew they could have been asking Joe if he had gone to church that day.

I kept smiling and quietly took cues from Joe. We moved into the dining room where the table had been set. Linen table-cloth, white china and cutlery that had belonged to his grand-mother were all laid out. As I sat and waited, I tried to take it all in. The aroma from the meal to come wafted temptingly from the kitchen. Joe's mom disappeared to tend to it as his dad continued to talk to Joe in Italian. With nothing but the delicious smells to distract me, all I could think about was eating.

Joe informed me that the cannelloni had been hand rolled and prepared by his mother. Each Sunday she followed the same routine. After Mass, she'd find her apron and return to the kitchen where her sauce had been simmering during their absence. The ritual of preparing lunch for her two men lasted three hours. The thought of that terrified me because I knew I was not that kind of Italian woman. Looking into the future, I was pretty certain I never would be that kind of Italian woman, nor would I ever want to become one. If this was going to be a prerequisite for parental approval, I could be in big trouble.

Mrs. Luciani finally emerged from the kitchen, platter in hand, and proudly presented the first course. The soup was delicious. Maybe the second bowl to which I helped myself wasn't strictly necessary, but you can never be sure what's to follow. As it turned out there were two choices of hand-made cannelloni: cheese or meat. Oh no! I hate choices. So I tried one of each. My belly was slowly expanding.

While I quietly enjoyed my little feast, the three of them chatted animatedly in a language that, despite my own proud Italian heritage, was unintelligible to me. (Well, I knew a bunch of swear words, but that hardly counts). Picking up no more than the occasional slang or single syllable word, I continued to take stock of this fabulous meal. The veal was cooked to perfection, and was especially tasty when paired with the oil and vinegar tossed salad. How wonderful to have a smorgasbord of my favourite dishes enticingly laid out before me, with no expectations for conversation (like those boring dinner parties), no fear of being interrogated (or given the shakedown as we like to call it), and certainly no insecurities about my table manners being critiqued. My mother would be proud. I drew no unnecessary attention to myself, I made no potentially embarrassing off-colour comments and I did my very best to demonstrate that Joe had indeed chosen a lovely girl.

Just as I was about to scoop a little bit more salad, I noticed Joe's dad lean over and said to Joe, "E meglio farti un vistito che farti una mangiata."

This time I knew something was up. Joe threw back his head and laughed. I stopped mid-chew, nervously inquiring what was so funny. Joe stopped chuckling long enough to offer the translation: "My father just warned me that it will be cheaper to keep you dressed in the finest of clothes than to keep you fed!"

Rather than be offended, I had to smile. He was right. I had eaten my way through that first meeting.

Before the deaths of Mr. and Mrs. Luciani there were many similar lunches, and without exception I enjoyed his mom's cooking immensely. The only difference from our first encounter was that over time we all made more of an effort to transcend the language barrier and communicate with each other.

Joe, however, is still desperately trying to keep me adequately clothed and fed.

One Size Does Not Fit All

One of the most enjoyable experiences I had in high school was being part of successful sports teams. I really didn't even have to try out because as soon as the coach laid eyes on me that first day of grade nine, I clearly had what she was looking for. I already measured 5'10".

It didn't matter that I had only ever touched a basketball once before (my brother tormented me so much about touching his things, I never tried it again). Somehow Miss Hughes knew there would be a spot for me. My role would be to plant myself and my size ten and a halfs right under our own basket. I didn't even have to shoot. All I was needed was to get the rebound and throw a long pass to one of the two very short forwards, who would most often drive to the hoop and score for the rest of us.

You can imagine how excited we were the day our new uniforms were scheduled to arrive. Our sizes had all been guesstimated, and what a range we were. The two allstar forwards, Cathy and Loretta were definite size sixes in perfect proportion to their petite 4'10" frames. The others ranged from size ten right up to my solo size sixteen.

It was a special day because right after we received our uniforms we were to pose for our team picture and then kick off our season on home court. Miss Hughes gathered us together and proudly presented each of us with our gold coloured tunic complete with our favourite number on the back. The tunic was to be worn over a freshly pressed short sleeved cotton blouse and navy blue cotton bloomers.

I secretly prayed that mine would fit.

Coveted garment in hand, we each headed off to one of the available corners of the change room. With considerable trepidation, I slipped out of my black serge uniform tunic into the newly manufactured gold one. Trying on a uniform was always difficult for me because I had never been a standard size. I still remember the embarrassment when I was eight, of my mother having to sew a reasonable facsimile skating costume for a year-end recital because the off-the-rack ones didn't fit over my chubby frame.

Minutes passed and I could hear my teammates enthusiastically enjoying their images in the mirror. They all sounded pleased with how they looked and definitely excited to get the season started. One by one I could hear them heading out of the locker room to the gym.

After a few minutes they realized I was the only one missing for the photo. I heard someone call, "C'mon Bertuzzi, what's taking you so long?"

Half laughing, half crying I shouted, "Where's the bottom?"

I could hear them laughing but I didn't budge.

My friend Carrie (forever the caring one) decided to follow the voice to find me and see what was taking so long. She spotted me in the back of the locker room bent forward and visibly shaking. Wondering what possibly could be the problem she came right up to me. I immediately pulled myself upright and turned to face her as the tears rolled down my face. I had laughed so hard I was crying.

I lowered my eyes and Carries' followed. The one-piece tunic had a fitted v-necked top with a two-buttoned section, which fit quite nicely over my starched white blouse. However, the lower pleated section of the one piece did not! Strangely, the pleats began just below my bustline like an empire waistline and ended somewhere between my belly button and my private parts (much like a pleated lamp shade). And hanging below like two flannel duffel bags were my navy blue bloomers.

Together, Carrie and I howled at the sight. We hugged as we shook with laughter; we cried; and we held our stomachs from the pain of the sudden eruption of emotion. We could not believe our eyes. As she protectively escorted me to the others, we enjoyed a collective roar of spontaneous laughter.

You see, the uniforms were all perfectly sized according to the width of our bodies. But somehow the lengths had all been measured to fit the two size six, 4'10" girls. Regardless of our height, all uniforms were made the same length.

We did manage to pose for our picture by leaning forward to create more length and I did play in the game but I wore an old tunic.

The season ended that year with us winning the championship and me wearing a perfectly fitted number thirteen, custom made for me ... by my mother.

I Coulda Been A Golfer

My brother and my dad used to golf together in the Niagara area. It was a new sport to the two of them and they were both quick to learn whatever they could about the game. As he pursued his new passion, my dad would often speak of Marlene Stewart-Streit, a local icon and one of Canada's most successful amateur female golfers. He was very impressed with her ability and felt honoured that they played the same course.

When our family moved to Mississauga, one of the first things my dad did was join a local cow pasture of a course. The price was right, it was within a mile of our home and he thought it had potential to develop into a pretty decent course. Interestingly, the course is Credit Valley, and true to my dad's prediction it ranks as one of the most beautifully laid-out courses with holes winding across and along the banks of the Credit River.

In 1962, the membership fee was low enough to afford and when they offered a considerably lower rate for kids, my dad quickly signed up my brother and sister. Being too young to join the club, I would tag along. And when no one was looking my dad would toss me a club and tell me to hit. Although I really wanted to swing as a leftie, my dad quickly changed that, directing me to ignore what was natural.

"Just forget about it and hit from the right like everyone else."

And hit I did. I had a lot of power and I could hit that ball every which way ... to the left, to the right, straight up and often out of sight completely. But every so often, I would connect and make that baby sail straight down the middle.

I don't really know how it happened but suddenly others were showing an interest in my ability.

"Hey, Carole, let me see you hit that ball."

"What club did you say you used on that one?"

"So you're the one people are talking about. I can see why!"

Having had no formal lessons, no success finding golf shoes that fit and using a club held together with a Band-Aid, I would continue to whack away at that ball.

Finally, when I was twelve I got my own membership. What followed were many nights going out on the course with my dad where he issued orders to me in hopes of teaching me the game.

"Don't baby it."

"Hit it like you mean it."

"Watch where you're aiming that thing."

"Slow down. Not so fast. It's not a race."

As I learned the game, he would entice me with wagers like: a nickel a hole, a dime a stroke and a quarter for the round. My dad's specialty was not the long ball but rather the short game. When I did manage to lace one off the tee, outdriving him by fifty yards he would smugly say, "We'll see who wins the hole."

As I flailed away, trying so hard to make contact with the ball and thus make good with my dad, I would inevitably be looking for it to land before I even hit it. This always drew the same demand from him.

"Keep your G*# damn head down."

And the more he yelled it, the harder it was for me to obey.

The summer I was twelve, I entered my first tournament, a cross club event at St. George's in Toronto. I was too young at the time to understand the greatness of the course and the history associated with it. What I do recall is standing on a tee on the back nine repeatedly hitting a ball into the water hazard in front. An older gentleman sat there watching in amusement. He said, "Don't worry honey. You just keep trying and one day you'll get it."

I laughed with him and said, "Yeah, I know. When I come back I'll be better."

Once I started playing regularly as a member of the club, arrangements were made for me to have lessons with the pro. Supposedly I showed tremendous potential and they all believed there could be some talent beneath the power.

I have one clear memory of the outings with the pro. He would put me in position with feet, grip and shoulders set. With cigarette dangling from the corner of his wrinkled and weathered mouth, he gripped a cold beer in one hand and in the other he gripped my head ... all in an effort to train me to keep my head down. I hit hundreds of balls from that position until it became routine to just step up to the ball and hit it.

When I was sixteen, I returned to St. George's, but this time it was for an invitational tournament attracting golfers from across Ontario. We were to tee off early morning but got rained out. Finally, it was rescheduled for an afternoon start. My friend Jim decided he would caddy for me. It remains in my mind as the purest golf game I have ever enjoyed. He handed me each club having already decided the right one to use, told me where to hit and the rest is recorded in history. I shot an eighty that game. I won the tournament. As I accepted the trophy, I thought of the elderly gentleman and wished I could see him again.

During that summer I played a lot of golf, hit a ton of

practice balls, endured numerous lessons and entered all of the tournaments. At the same time, though, I was enjoying a part time job at the candy counter at Kresge's, playing on a baseball team, hanging out at the tennis courts with my friends and trying to enjoy every second of my summer as a teenager. I was doing it all and loving it.

Each summer after that, however, the pressure to do well in golf increased. Every day my dad would check in to see if I had practised, asked what I had shot and what my handicap was. I found myself lying to him and sneaking off the course early to be with my friends. I still entered the tournaments but it really was for the enjoyment of hanging out with the other golfers and being away from home. The golf came third.

It was developing into a source of angst for all of us as the rest of the family witnessed the close scrutiny I was under by both my dad and other members of the club. The worst part was that they'd publish scores in the local paper for all to read and remember so I couldn't even fabricate them. This half-hearted devotion to a sport that I was destined to succeed in (by everyone else's standards) continued until I was nineteen.

One day in May, I was entered in a tournament in Etobicoke. I experienced the customary first tee nervousness and started the game with my three opponents. As I typically did, I kept score in my head according to five's, shooting a six meant 'one over', a four was 'one under'. By the third hole my mind was already racing ahead to the fourth, knowing I needed to birdie it to stay even. Instead, I had a double bogey. By the fifth hole, I was really putting the pressure on myself. Desperate thoughts consumed me. How could I possibly finish the front nine with a respectable score?

And then it happened. Like having the lights go out in my mind, I short-circuited. My arms went limp, my body weakened and I could not move. I thought I might pass out, so I just stood there trying to regain my composure. Within minutes, as the others hovered around me, I summoned the little energy I had left in me and announced, "I think I better go in."

I believed I was having a nervous breakdown from the self-imposed pressure to do well ... for my dad.

I slowly headed back to the clubhouse with little recognition of my whereabouts. Wearily I approached the registration table and informed them that I would not be continuing. I went into the clubhouse, called home and asked for someone to pick me up. When my mom arrived, she took one look at me and realized it was best not to quiz me. All she said was, "Are you okay? We'll tell your dad together."

As I nervously shared the incident with my dad later in the day, I followed it up with, "I can't play anymore. You want it more than I do. I'm sorry."

No big heated argument followed. He didn't really have much to say. He didn't have to. I knew what he was feeling ... I was wasting my God given athletic ability; I was squandering an opportunity to succeed in a sport that was opening up for women thanks to the likes of Marlene Stewart-Streit and I was tossing aside a dream, albeit his.

It took us a few years to get our relationship back on track. I never entered another tournament. I rarely picked up a club, but when I did, the comments were immediate once again.

"My God woman, can you hit that ball!"

"Did you ever think of taking golf up seriously?"

"Wow, had you applied yourself, you could have been a golfer."

My dad and I refrained from golfing together for twenty years. It was too painful. Finally, when he turned seventy, I gave him a gift ... five golf games with me to be played that summer. I knew the time was right and that it was something he'd appreciate.

We continued this annual gift tradition until his death at eighty. Although he never openly admitted it, I know my dad enjoyed those games. Invariably the starter would think we were a married couple because of my own silver hair. My dad would get a chuckle out of that because he knew it would rattle me so much that it would throw me off my game for the first few holes.

The banter was non-stop. He'd call out, "Nice hit, Ida" (referring to my mother, who has never swung a club in her life) after I'd make a bad shot. Bending over to retrieve the ball after sinking the putt, or in a lot of cases the chip, he'd look up and with a wink, he'd say, "Hah. I'm pretty sure I beat ya." And after most games I'd owe him at least $1.50.

I play for fun now. I miss those games with my dad. We never talked about my early days again, but I think of them often. Especially when I shank one and shudder as I hear his voice boom out, "Keep your G%^ damn head down."

P.S. For my dad's seventy-fifth birthday I gave him a book called Once Upon a Lifetime. In it was a list of questions for him to answer. Opening this gift he griped, "When the hell am I going to have the time to do this?"

Five years later, shortly after his death, I came across the book. He had found the time to answer every question ... complete with attachments. One answer caught my eye. Responding to the question, 'When you were younger, what did you aspire to be when you grew up?'

He wrote, 'I wanted to be involved in sports'.

My Day at the Spa

My friends must have known I needed a little pampering when they presented me with a coupon for a half day at a world famous European spa in the city. I was retiring from my job at the hospital before the birth of my second child. It was a good thing the coupon had a one-year expiry date because it certainly took me that long to get the courage to go.

I have always been somewhat intimidated by atmospheres of glamour and sophistication. I wear hardly any makeup. In fact, the only blush I wore for eight years was from the compact that Joe's first wife left behind in the cabinet. I had never been one to have my nails done. Probably because, prior to the invention of gel nails (of which I have become a firm devotee), there was rarely enough of a nail left to do anything with. And to that point in my life, my idea of relaxation was riding the stationery bike, cordless phone to ear, watching *Oprah* as baby Dante rode bareback on my bouncing knee. I wasn't into the spa scene at all.

Six months later, I felt ready to enjoy the thoughtful gift from my friends. I was actually a little excited about having my whims and wishes gratified. I even arranged for Joe to take me out to some place special that evening so that the results of the day would not be wasted. I would even dress up.

Approaching the reception desk, I had already scanned the waiting room. Stepford wives, Barbie dolls and chic ur-

ban looking women eyed me back. Somehow, my post pregnancy stretch pants and desert boots seemed a little out of
place. I took my seat and studied each one carefully. They all
seemed so casually elegant and poised as they flipped through
the pages of *Toronto Life* and *Cosmopolitan*. I dared not take the
worn and tattered *Dr. Spock* out of the old net bag that I toted
everywhere.

Finally, a crisp looking woman with hair so tightly pulled
back that it created a wonderful face-lift illusion approached
me. She spoke a brand of English I could not comprehend. I
got up, and with head tilted towards her in order to maximize
my chances of hearing and understanding her better, I followed closely on her heels. No small talk. I kept quiet. I would
hate to miss a valuable directive. She led me to a curtained
cubicle, handed me a towel-type garment, and left. Thanks,
lady, for your warm and friendly welcome. I feel so much more
comfortable now.

Drawing the curtain, I began to undress. I looked at the
garment. Hmm. Might this only be a towel? Nah, it's got snaps.
I maneuvered it around my body. If I got it to cover the bottom portion, it revealed my boobs. If I covered my top, my
privates were revealed. It was a dilemma. I peaked out from
behind the curtain and waved for her attention. Stepping out,
I wordlessly demonstrated how the item just did not seem to
measure up (literally). Her only response was a snicker from
behind her beautifully manicured hand. Making the best of it,
I crouched down to cover as much of myself as possible, and
shuffled out to the open area.

I followed the iron maiden, hunchback style, to a dimly
lit room. The scent of lavender filled the air and soft music
played from the tape deck in the corner. I then faced a Nordic
woman of weightlifter stature whose English also confounded
me. She directed me to the table where I would receive my
first-ever massage. Not knowing what to expect I tried to get
lost in my thoughts. Her hands were strong. She kneaded my
skin with the force of a car being pushed out of a snow bank.

Moving from one limb to another she systematically loosened the knots beneath her grip. Surprisingly, it felt pretty good.

Until she started to rub my breasts. Aaaaaaaaagh! Was this part of it? Was I supposed to enjoy this? My eyes darted to hers. She was really getting into it, kneading the flesh with her fingers. I curled my mouth into a snarl. She smiled. This language barrier was proving to be a real pain. Tensing up from foot to forehead, I endured the rest of the treatment in tortured silence. Maybe, I thought, I'm being naive. Don't make a big deal. It's the European way I'm sure. I faked sleep.

My next treatment was a facial. Knowing by now that any attempt at humour was likely to be ignored or misunderstood, I decided to just sit back and enjoy it. The esthetician's hands were hypnotic, and I allowed myself to relax into the rejuvenating treatment. When it came time for my manicure and pedicure, I had a new decision to make, because now I was face-to-face with the technician handling my extremities. Talk or don't talk? When I'm uncomfortable I try to chat, so I found myself diving in despite my better judgment. No response. I sat there staring at the dyed roots of her scalp. Geez, I was hoping to have more fun today.

Arriving for the makeup session, I was relieved to discover the fellow spoke a language I could understand. Ah, I could finally have a conversation. He asked me about my preference for 'looks'... like I know this? He was interested in knowing what kind of make-up I used. I was too embarrassed to tell him about the inherited blush and that my main skin lotion to date had been Johnson's Baby Cream. When he asked me what I was looking for I told him I was really hoping for a natural look. Surely, I thought, it was possible to have my makeup professionally done, feel comfortable with it, and still be recognizable to Joe.

The facial had cleansed my skin, opened my pores and left my face sparkling. And now, I had to prepare myself for the fact that all this goodness had to be covered over. Staring at the assortment of creams, powders and paints in front of me, I wished I could escape. He started. Foundation was evenly dabbed over my entire face and neck. As it tightened, I felt my skin pull. If nothing else, I too might look like I had benefited from a lift. Eye shadow was layered in three tones above my eye. This virgin area whined its disapproval. The mascara was brushed in four directions over my previously angel hair lashes. Blush was then applied to accent my cheekbones. My thin lips were outlined to appear fuller and the lipstick coloured in. A quick brush over with the powder puff and I wanted to cry.

I looked at my reflection in the mirror and I couldn't believe how awful I looked. Who was this painted woman? I didn't know whether I looked like a scary Halloween mask or a clown prepared for a day at the Santa Claus parade. I nodded my thanks, and with lowered eyes, I quickly left the spa, hoping against hope that I wouldn't run into someone I knew.

I couldn't get back to the van soon enough. Whipping the door open I began a mad search for the baby wipes. Without so much as a quick glance in the mirror to make sure that my revulsion was indeed justified, I whitewashed my entire face. Wipe after wipe, I began to feel the mask lift and my spirits with it. Once the last trace of guck was finally off my face and neck, I felt positively buoyant. From the mirror, my fresh sparkling face stared back. Ahh … so much better.

Driving home, I laughed at my own insecurities. This pampering thing maybe wasn't for me after all. When I got home, Joe didn't notice I looked any different than when I had left that morning, which was fine by me. To celebrate my new beauty (inner, that is), we scrapped the fancy restaurant idea and ordered a pizza. We enjoyed ourselves immensely.

Whenever I get the chance, I still ask people about their massage experiences. As they recount their stories with pleasure, I listen intently while they describe the details of their treatment. When I casually ask if the therapist ever massages 'uncharted territory' they shout, "No! Are you kidding? I'd die."

Without going into specifics, I find myself thinking that perhaps I wasn't the one whose whims and wishes were most gratified that day.

How A Child Deals with Difficult People

It was always difficult to prepare for my presentations as I busily parented my young children. The fall that Dante turned three, I remember one night when I made a rushed attempt to put him to bed. Impatiently, with lots on my mind, I took the liberty of reading the shortened, self edited version of the bedtime story, slurred the evening prayer and hastily responded to his questions that demanded answers.

I kept repeating, "C'mon Honey, Mommy has to go and do some work," hoping this mini version of an adult could somehow comprehend the importance of my plea. But it only prolonged the procedure.

Dante asked, "What kind of work, Mommy?"

As best I could, I tried to explain, "Dante, Mommy needs to do some work because tomorrow morning after we wake up, I have to go some place and talk to some people."

"What kind of people, Mommy?"

"Well, remember when we took you to the hospital for stitches and those nice people took care of you? I'm going to talk to people like them, who also work in a hospital."

"What are you going to talk about?"

Hmm, this was getting more tedious than I had time for. "Dante, you know sometimes when someone does something that bothers you? Um, you know, who annoys you or really bugs you? Like when Vincie makes you angry?"

"Yeah."

"Well, Dante, I'm going to talk about what they can do when this happens. Honey, what would you do if someone was bothering you?"

Thinking long and hard about this one and trying to buy as much time as possible, Dante finally came up with his own tips for 'dealing with difficult people'.

He started: "I would spank them on their bum to make them stop."

Not overly pleased to hear this, I kept silent. I know that spanking is futile because it only hurts your hand.

Dante continued. "No, I would call the police and have them take them away."

Okay, now I knew he would not take the law into his own hands.

Still not satisfied, he was quick to add, "I know. I'll take them to the zoo and have the lions eat them."

Ouch. Obviously, my face mirrored my thoughts.

Sensing it was time to mellow up, Dante came up with yet another technique. "No, Mommy, I would take them to the airport and let them fly away."

I smiled. At least it was a peaceful solution.

As I found myself enjoying this serendipitous conversation I realized just how much I could learn from my children ... if I only gave them the chance to teach me. I sighed with affection in my eyes and he made one last attempt to keep my attention.

He started to smile and giggled, "I know, Mommy, I would tickle them until they started to laugh!"

I knew then, at any time, Dante could fill my shoes. In less than five minutes, he had outlined five different ways to handle an annoying person. Some not suitable, some too painful and some that could serve us all well. I kissed him goodnight knowing I had the opening for the next day's session.

Psyched Out

It was sheer persistence and optimism that earned me a spot on the registrar's admission list for Fall 1971 at the University of Waterloo. At the end of August of that year it appeared that I would not be going to university as planned, as I had not been accepted anywhere I had applied. It wasn't because I wasn't smart enough, although I do admit to not putting out much of an effort during high school. It was because I had missed writing the necessary exams while I spent thirty-two days in isolation at South Peel (now Trillium) Hospital recovering from knee surgery.

The rejection letters did not deter me. The Friday before Labour Day, I decided that attending university was not an experience I was going to miss. It didn't take long to pack up my only suitcase because having worn a uniform throughout high school, I didn't have a lot of clothes. Of course, my parents were concerned and they had a long list of reasonable questions for me. I assured them I would be fine. I was a big girl and I would somehow make it work.

I arrived on campus as nothing more than an unofficial guest, and took turns bunking in with various friends. This gave me a great opportunity to meet all kinds of people and test out different residences. Every morning I checked in with the registrar's office to see if my application had been accepted; afternoons were for practising flag football and evenings for partying with my new friends. I was having a blast. I was captain of the flag team and had been elected floor rep in a residence where I didn't even have a room.

My persistence paid off. In the third week of the first semester, I learned that my application had officially been accepted. A week after that I managed to get a room in residence. Despite all odds, it was shaping up to be a great year.

Like most other first year students, it took until Thanksgiving to get used to the idea of my newly acquired freedom. It felt like being at camp, only there were no rules to follow. Our top priority each day was to spend as much time together as we could, and have as much fun as possible. Class attendance was reluctantly squeezed into our busy schedules.

My most memorable course that first semester was Psychology 101. The professor must have been handpicked to appeal to this hormonally charged group of three hundred first year students because he did an amazing job of keeping us interested. His body darted about the stage in harmony with the passion of his statements. His theatrical presentation each Tuesday kept us engaged enough to want to return on Thursday. He introduced us to theories that I remember to this day. There was Pavlov's Dog, Skinner's Theory of Operant Conditioning, and Maslow's Hierarchy of Needs. We were fascinated by the characteristics of the many personality disorders, each of us secretly trying to identify our own afflictions. I couldn't remember the last time I had been so interested in learning.

I was not concerned when our professor announced the date of our mid-term, the first mid-term of my university career. He told us what chapters to study and indicated how long we would have to complete the test. He advised us that the format would be one hundred multiple-choice questions, and concluded the overview by assuring us that we didn't have to get all worked up about it. He had given the test to a monkey. The monkey had scored twenty-eight. We all chuckled our way out of class.

During the next few nights, whenever I tried to study for

the test, I was always coaxed back to the 'fun on the floor'. It didn't take much to convince me that if a monkey could get a mark of twenty-eight, I had nothing to worry about. Besides, everyone knew that 'multiple guess' was easier than essay style.

By test day, I was confident. Sharpened pencil in hand, I attacked the ten pages of questions, never forgetting the theory: 'when in doubt, pick c'. It certainly didn't appear to be difficult, however a few of the questions were vague enough to be confusing. I finished on time and confidently handed in my test. I then forgot about it until the day he showed up at class with two shopping bags full of the marked papers.

Naturally, the sight of them made my belly churn. My thoughts darted back to the days of elementary school when, after hearing your name called, you would work your way to the front of the room, sneak a peek at the upper right corner of the paper for the mark, gasp, turn purple and then ignore all whispers of "What'd ya get?" as you made your way back to your seat to collapse. At least that's what it was like for us weaker students.

Well, the moment of truth was drawing near and soon I would know the outcome of my first university test experience. This would surely set the tone for my academic future. Like a drill sergeant, the prof belted out the surname on each of the papers. Upon hearing our names, we jumped up and quickly stepped into line to retrieve our paper as though we had been ordered 'to keep the kettle boiling'. I heard my name and took my place in line. Just then, he decided to remind us about the monkey's success and to inform us that three students among us were hovering just above monkey status. I was now even more afraid to look. I purposely didn't curl back the marked corner until I was back in my seat. My friends leaned closer to catch a peek. It was time.

In large red numbers with three scratches below for emphasis stood the offending score: thirty-two. I had beaten the monkey ... but just by four points. I went numb. I was embarrassed. The teasing was incessant. That evening, the bunches of bananas left at the door of my room were painful reminders of my performance.

Although I never forgot the monkey I did manage to get over what happened, and even learned a little bit about the value of 'smart' studying along the way. I passed Psych 101 with a mark of seventy-two that first semester … and continued to have the time of my life.

PS. A few years later when I was teaching my first high school class, I shared the story with my students. I'll always treasure the monkey cookie jar they gave me as a reminder of the lesson.

For A Good Time Wear ...

When parents go on vacation they often bring back something for their kids as a souvenir of the trip, like a t-shirt or something that represents the area they visited. Every tourist destination has its fair share of kitsch that visitors seem eager to buy. When my own parents visited Hawaii in 1973, my mom bought me two pairs of socks. They arrived in the mail while I was away at school.

This may seem like a trivial gift, but my mom knew this about me: I love socks. I believe it's because they are far more easy to buy than any other piece of clothing. The wilder and more interesting the design, the more I welcome them into my sock drawer. However, these Hawaiian socks did not quite meet even my standards. I wasn't really attracted to the design, nor did they feel that great. Made from one hundred percent nylon, I was sure my feet would sweat excessively. The colours were ever so 70's, in beige, white and brown for the first pair and pale blue, white and navy for the second. The design was a floral pattern that seemed to repeat itself ad nauseam. They were not, as my mother thought, 'all the go'. They were ugly.

After studying each pair in horror, I decided I could probably have some fun with them. Always optimistic, I decided right then to not only wear them but to turn them into my 'good time socks'. I had corduroy pants to match each pair and whenever I was ready to go out partying with friends (this occurred quite regularly in those days), I would be sure to include them as accessories. Within a short time, friends caught on to my plan and these socks became an integral part my social life. We had become good friends. They started to mold to my foot. They were comfortable, and whenever I wore them I was sure to have a good time as planned.

The next year, when I was ready to leave on a four-month trip I did not have to think very long about what I would pack. The socks were the first items to claim a spot in the bottom of my knapsack. I knew they would guarantee a memorable trip across the country.

We covered a lot of ground in North America that fall, and eventually we arrived in Vancouver. One evening, my friend Nancy and I went out for a Chinese meal in a place called the Varsity Grill. As we sat there planning the next leg of our trip, I occasionally glanced around the restaurant to keep my people-watching skills sharp. In the front corner of the restaurant, I caught a glimpse of something that made me lean closer and squint for a clearer view. I could not believe what I was seeing. Under the table, in a pair of Wallabees, were a pair of socks identical to my own 'good time' pair. After looking down at my feet to make sure my own beloved socks were where they should be, I immediately jumped up from my seat.

I howled with pleasure at the coincidence. Nancy's face registered concern as my body contorted and I sucked back the air as I laughed. I was enjoying the kind of laugh that takes a minute before you come up for air. Hoisting up my pant legs, I shuffled over to the stranger in the corner. I was giddy with delight as my mouth hung open, still gasping for air. By the time I got to his table, I had all but lost control, and was oblivious to the impression I was making on him and his friends. All I could do was tug on his shirt with this stupid look on my face and point to my ankles. He looked in amazement at the vision before him. We were wearing the same hideous socks!

His screwed up expression sent me into a renewed spasm of chortles, and it took a few moments to compose myself enough to recite my story (See, I've been a story teller forever). He listened with great pleasure and when I finally stopped to take a breath, he jumped in and told me that he, too, had gotten his socks in Hawaii, chosen lovingly for their pure tackiness.

When Nancy finally figured out what was going on, she came over and joined us.

The party had started. The socks had come through yet again.

Hotel Hospitality?

One late summer day in 1983, Joe and I were enjoying the final leg of a five-day bicycle trip. Hot, grimy and exhausted, we decided to treat ourselves to a more luxurious accommodation than we had allowed ourselves on previous nights. The first four nights had been spent in what could be characterized as High 'n Low Efficiency Units, with the emphasis on low. After considering a few nice places along the lake in Kingston, we eventually booked into one of the two major hotel chains. When the young man behind the counter quoted our beyond-the-budget rate, we both nodded, agreeing that it would be worth it.

We squeezed into the elevator with bikes in tow and watched the floor numbers change. We were too tired to talk. We had been married long enough to know that ongoing chatter was not always necessary nor appreciated. Silently, we each mapped out what we would do when we got to the room. Wheeling our bikes along the corridor, we announced our intentions to each other. Joe declared he was ready for a snooze. I was set on a long shower to wash away the dust and dirt and to massage my aching body after the day's forty-mile ride.

As soon as we entered the room and parked the bikes out of the way, Joe was off. First with his clothes and then to his 'ahh, this feels good' position, sprawled out naked on the bed. It took about three and a half seconds before he was snoring with gusto.

Focusing on getting to my own destination, I stood just outside the bathroom door yanking the damp clothing from my body. I was down to my last piece, when I heard what sounded an awful lot like a key turning in our door. Panic pierced through me. I tossed a whisper out, loud enough for Joe to hear. "Joe, I think someone's trying to get into our room."

Without missing a wink of his nap, he assured me that the sound was probably coming from across the hall.

Hesitantly, I sighed and yanked off the last sock. But then I heard the sound again, only this time I could see the door handle move. AGGGGGGHHHHH !! Before I could reach for cover, the door opened and there before me stood a family of four. The man, and imposing figure in a military uniform, carried the family's luggage. His wife cringed at the sight of us and carefully shielded the two children who peaked out from behind her legs. Obviously, none of them had been expecting to walk in on a scene like this.

Joe lay naked on the bed, pretending he was dead. The only parts that had moved were his arms, which had found the 'home plate' position to cover up his private parts. He told me later that he had figured if he was quiet and still they might not notice him.

By contrast, I had accepted my fate head on. At least that's where I hoped they would cast their eyes because like Joe, I too was now naked. All of those *Dressing for Success* and *Power of Nonverbal Communication* seminars suddenly took on new meaning for me. There I stood attempting desperately to cover my oversized body with my undersized arms. With no room for gesturing I feebly uttered, "Excuse me, but this is our room."

The man looked right at me and bellowed angrily, "Well, there must be some mistake because I've got the key." As if to underscore his point, he thrust it in my direction.

"Bu-but, I've got the key too and we were here first."

He looked around the room one more time and glaring disgustedly at me (maybe I should have shaved my legs after all), he turned and ushered his wilted family towards the door, muttering that he was going to take the matter up with the front desk. His final declaration was, "We'll be back."

As I stared at the back of his head, I replied, "That's fine. But please knock first."

With the click of the closing door behind them, Joe revived himself and together we let out a momentous shriek. We rolled over in fits of laughter, the absurdity of the situation overriding our considerable mutual embarrassment.

To our great relief, they did not return.

That evening when Joe and I were leaving the hotel for dinner, I decided I should speak to someone at the front desk about the incident. After all, customer service was one of my areas of expertise and I felt they deserved to hear how we felt about what had happened. I approached the counter and made my intro.

"Uh, yes, I would like to express my disappointment about an awkward situation that went on in our room earlier today." I purposely remained vague.

The young man behind the front desk met my gaze and it was apparent that my story had preceded me because with no trace of concern, he interrupted, "Oh yeah. Man, I was so embarrassed."

"You were embarrassed? We were the ones without any clothes on."

His 'I really don't care' attitude made my blood boil. At that moment, we knew that customer satisfaction was not a priority, nor a specialty of this chain of hotels. I demanded to see the manager.

Fortunately, he got the message and offered us compensation. This gesture settled me down and as we shook hands I took comfort in getting the last word.

"Thanks, but next time we'll be going to the hotel that promises no surprises."

Shoulda Proofread

$\mathcal{G}$oing off to St. Joe's High School wasn't overly exciting for me because I was merely following in my sister's footsteps and her perfect steps had been notoriously hard to follow my entire life. I had no choice though, because this was where Bertuzzi children went to high school. I was fitted for my uniform, the white blouses were purchased and the black oxfords specially ordered in size eleven. I was not looking forward to wearing this heavy black tunic ensemble, especially in the hot weather. Reluctantly I stepped off the bus that first day. If only I knew then the positive impact those five years would have on my life, I may have had more spring in my step.

That first week was not uneventful. Caught tossing my 'beanie' onto the head of the statue of St. Joseph in the yard did not go unnoticed. On only my third day of grade nine, I was caught monkeying around in the hallway outside a very important assembly for the older students. For that I was granted a one-week detention. The principal did not pass up the opportunity to remind me that my grade eight teacher had warned her about my reckless behaviour. I was mortified by both her comment and the unfair report from my past teacher. When she told me that she had prepared all of my teachers ahead of time, I knew I was a marked student.

From then on, I tried to keep my distance from trouble, or at least not get caught. Other than the occasional uniform blunder or faking sick to miss a test, I was generally well be-haved enough to escape reprimand. Sure, I once got caught hiding in a closet during science class, and on most days could be seen mimicking the school's ancient librarian as she shuffled to the library door, key in hand searching for the keyhole. But I was harmless. Honest.

It didn't take long for me to make my mark with the stu-dent body either. While my teachers regarded me with extreme wariness, my peers embraced me. I knew most everyone in the school. I played on all the teams and I guess you could say I had a bit of a reputation. So, by the time spring rolled around I was feeling pretty comfortable there. It was student council election time and I decided to follow the tradition created by my brother and sister before me and to run for office. I would vie for the position of sports rep, and my theme would be the Jolly Green Giant. I thought it was appropriate; I was the tall-est girl in the school when I stood up straight and, since I loved a good time, jolly was suitable. Besides, the next year we would start to wear our new putrid olive green blazers and kilts. I couldn't miss with this theme.

It happened that we had a close family friend, Bill, who took an active role in our lives. He liked to get involved in our interests. When I told him of my plans he was more than en-couraging. He was excited about helping yet a third Bertuzzi to an election victory.

Bill advised me: "Carole, let me write your campaign speech. You concentrate on the poster side of things and the day-to-day drumming up of votes." I thought this was a great idea since the speech part was already making me nervous. With Kathe as my campaign manager (note: this spelling of her name is not a typo ... Kathe chose this as one method of distinguishing herself from the rest of the bunch, although she was no slouch in the behaviour department either), my election team was now complete. Kathe even wrote a catchy song about me which drew a lot of attention when, accompanied by her guitar, she belted it out in the busy hallways between classes.

Election week was a whirl of frenzy. We handed out Green Giant bookmarks, had poster parties and anxiously schemed how to acquire the best spots for hanging them. I was elated when our mad dash succeeded in squeezing out others for the prime spot: dropping over the balcony into the gymnasium.

On Friday afternoon just before the assembly, Bill met me outside of the gym, speech in hand. He pulled me aside and proceeded to give me strict instructions on how to deliver it. "Carole, this is the most important part of your campaign. I want you to go in there and find a friendly face. Talk to that face. With this speech, you're going to win their hearts and their votes."

Bill handed the paper over to me. He had highlighted the important parts: when to pause and what to stress. Since I had not been given the opportunity to practise the speech before the assembly began, I had to believe that I could summon up what it would take to deliver it effectively. My stomach whirling with butterflies, I entered the gymnasium.

All the candidates were seated across the front of the stage, overlooking the packed room. I couldn't keep my knees from knocking. One by one, each candidate was invited to the microphone to deliver her speech, and I tried to pay attention as they made their respective promises.

Finally, I heard my name called. Getting up, I searched for that friendly face. I couldn't find one. The room was a massive blur of black and white. In the front four rows sat the lay teaching staff and the nuns in their starched black cloth and white cardboard habits. All six hundred students, squirming in their own black and white uniforms, occupied the thirty rows behind them. I quickly decided it might be best to speak to the back wall (that way everyone figures you're looking at someone behind them). Gripping the speech in my sweaty palms, I began, "Sisters, teachers and fellow students. Don't be concerned that the Jolly Green Giant only wears leaves. (Breathe). Just keep in mind that Eve only wore leaves too." (Pause). Faces twisted at the biblical reference. Raising a long index finger in the air to make the next point, I continued, "Now I know why Adam's favourite season was fall!"

Reading it for the first time, even I was surprised by the raciness of the joke (remember, these were infinitely more innocent times), but my surprise paled in comparison to the disbelief that registered in the eyes before me. As I looked out onto the floor below, I knew that it didn't matter what was contained in the rest of the speech. This was the only part they would remember. The front four rows of nuns were trying desperately to keep a lid on their emotions. They were really trying to hold it in, biting their lips and holding their breath to keep the snorts and laughter from escaping. In the thirty rows behind the staff, a ruckus had definitely been created by my words and nobody from that crowd was trying to hold it in. Students from all grades were hootin' and hollerin'. Someone yelled out, "Bertuzzi, I can't believe you said that!"

They whistled and howled for me to continue. No sooner did I reach my conclusion and challenge them with my slogan: "So, please be choosey, vote Bertuzzi!" then I knew I was doomed.

From the corner of my eye, I watched as the principal worked her way out the door. I hoped that maybe she just needed some respite from the heat that had hung in the gym. As I moved off the stage to thunderous applause and stomping of oxfords on floor, I could faintly hear a familiar sound. Oh no, my instincts were right ... the swinging rosary beads were headed my way.

As we collided, Sister reached out and gripped my arm. With no exchange of words, she escorted me to the entrance of the chapel. Once there, with the power of the statues behind her and still squeezing my arm, Sister put her finger to my face and started her rant. "That was disgusting. That was humiliating. I have every notion to expel you this minute. Let me remind you that I have only tolerated you because of your sister Sharon, who has never caused us any trouble."

Pulse racing and fear gripping my stomach, I looked down

at her and shamelessly groveled, "Oh, Sister. I didn't think it was funny either. Someone else wrote that speech for me, Sister. Honest. You know me, I would never say anything like THAT."

Sure, I was grasping for life support but what else could I say? She loosened her grip on me and left me standing alone and feeling defeated at the chapel entrance. The sweetness of the week had suddenly soured but at least I had narrowly managed to save myself once again.

Well, that day I did win their hearts and yes, their votes. But I learned a very valuable lesson from that experience. I had attempted to use someone else's idea of humour and had nearly paid a very dear price. I had offended the principal and she was the one who held the future of my education in the palm of her hands. That day I realized that humour is also in the eyes of the beholder and that going for the laugh is sometimes just not worth the risk.

The Sunday Sermon

When we were children our dad was constantly trying to improve himself by reading, attending conventions and taking courses. He believed the best thing he ever did for himself was to enroll in a *Dale Carnegie* course in 1961. Because of the demands of his work, community, church and family commitments, the only opportunity he had to practise his weekly lesson was on Sunday morning before Mass. Typically, he would order us away from the black and white cartoons we were watching on TV and direct us to take a seat at the kitchen table. We would pour our bowls of cereal and take our positions. There he stood, across the table, silently waiting and poised to deliver the communication tip of the week.

Unfortunately, such valuable lessons were all but wasted on our young ears. He had our attention more out of fear than of interest. We were afraid to take our eyes off of our dad because doing so might stir the lion within. So, we sat in silence as we munched away. We devoured our breakfast as quietly as we could, waiting and watching my dad as he prepared to address his audience.

One such Sunday, attired in dress pants and undershirt, Dad loomed over us from the other side of the table, his stern eyes staring directly at us. As we grew restless in anticipation, he reached to his right and picked up a recent edition of The *St. Catharine's Standard*. We fidgeted as the silence lengthened.

Continuing to stare us down, he slowly and methodically began rolling the paper into a tight cylinder. With a firm grip on the resulting weapon, he leered at each one of us, eyeball to eyeball, making certain we were with him. Then, with a force that could squash a tarantula, he wound up and hit the edge of the table so hard the milk in our cereal bowls went flying. With bulging eyes and cowering bodies, we watched our dad in fear of what might follow. Then, convinced he had us, he pointed at each of us in turn with his other index finger and proclaimed, "First, you have to get their attention."

My dad did get our attention that day ... and many days after that. He never tired of trying to get his point across to us in his authoritarian manner or of sharing some essential wisdom.

The first and only time my dad heard me speak professionally, his comments were brief. "You're not too bad. I still think you should consider taking the *Dale Carnegie Course.*"

Although I never did enroll in the course to enhance my own public speaking, thanks to my dad I will never forget the lessons of those Sunday mornings in 1961 ... especially the importance of 'getting their attention'.

Nice Butt, But...

Tennis has always been a passion of mine. As an avid player, I was determined to play throughout my first pregnancy. I especially enjoyed playing on the club team in the Inter-County League. It guaranteed good tennis, good food and every once in a while, good company. Rarely, though, would I benefit from a good laugh. It was far too serious for that.

One evening in July of 1985, I sat around waiting for my match to begin. I had chosen to sit rather than stand because I was already in my eighth month. Although it hadn't done wonders for my figure, I sure could deliver a mean overhead with all the extra weight. As I waited, I enjoyed watching the other matches on the front courts.

On beautiful nights in the summer, the club was a popular spot. On this evening, there were lots of people milling about and relaxing on the deck around me. I remember getting up to check who my partner would be for my next match. I was told it would be John. I couldn't recall who John was, so my captain described him to me. Oh, yes. I remembered then that handsome young guy with the great smile and nice buns. Yes, when women get together, we do chat about such things.

I went back to my seat feeling a bit self-conscious, knowing that I would be playing with such a handsome young man. Suddenly I didn't feel very attractive as I looked down at the inner tube that seemed to have wrapped itself around my middle

... all forty-eight pounds of it by that time. Moreover, maybe it wasn't the best night to have borrowed Joe's XL sweatshirt and flannel shorts. I felt frumpy and dumpy ... and just the thought of it made me grumpy.

As I sat there wishing we could get out on the court and get it over with, I sensed someone approach me. I looked up and there stood my partner. He really was a good-looking man. He smiled a broad grin and introduced himself. I was captured by his charm. As I maneuvered the tennis bag on my lap in an unsuccessful attempt to hide my bulk, we chatted and I expressed my keenness to play our match. After a few moments he wandered away to pass the remaining time.

As he walked away from me, I couldn't help but follow him with my eyes. A brief glance to his butt and I saw what looked to be an opening in the seam of his pants. I know, what was I doing looking there anyway? Well I always like to 'take it all in' and this was one situation that definitely merited the attention. He stopped at the railing and hoisted up one leg to lean on as he watched the matches below. I squinted harder. I was certain, no doubt about it, that was his butt exposed to the early evening light.

I gripped the edges of my deck chair. Ouch, what a vision! The poor guy. I waited and watched, wishing that any second he would clue in to his predicament. But clearly he did not because he proceeded to drop his leg, jam his hands in his pockets and rock from toe to heel, heel to toe. Oh dear! The ripped seam was now opening and closing like a change purse.

Time passed and more and more people were catching on. It amazed me that so many could sit back and snicker behind their hands at this scene, yet no one was prepared to do anything to save this poor young man. Even me. All eyes still on him, he took a seat that had been vacated nearby. Whew! I thought for sure this would finally be his moment to recognize the bare facts. After all, that seat must have felt cooler than usual on his sculpted behind.

But still no reaction from him. As many of the onlookers giggled, some started to goad me into doing something about it. I wondered why I had been the designated snitch. They argued that it was because I was his partner. Sure, and I guess it didn't matter that I had met him for the first time not ten minutes earlier. I cringed at the thought of the embarrassment this might cause us both. But my qualms were replaced by determination when he got up and started pacing back and forth in front of us, widening the tear with every step. I looked around; everyone on the entire deck had fixed their eyes on his bare butt, which surely must have been feeling the night breeze by then. Enough already! This had to be stopped, and the responsibility had clearly fallen on me.

I got up and walked towards him. As we stood side by side, with eyes staring off into the night, I leaned toward him and whispered, "Uh, John, I'm sure you're not aware of this but the seam of your tennis shorts appears to have come apart. You might want to check it out."

His hand immediately jerked to his backside. As he looked straight ahead, his face crinkled up and he elaborately mouthed the words, "Ohhh, no."

I slowly removed the borrowed sweatshirt, which I now was thankful to have brought, and passed it wordlessly to him. Unaware that all eyes were on us, he wrapped it around his waist as one might casually drape a sweater over chilly shoulders on a cool night. He turned to go, assured that his dignity was intact. Little did he know that his backside now bore the words PROPERTY OF NOTRE DAME in five-inch golden letters.

When I returned home that night, Joe wondered about the absence of his favourite sweatshirt. The explanation came easily. "I had to save a guy's butt."

The Power of Pink

$\mathcal{E}$ ver since meeting Joe in 1976, I have taken to the sidelines as he pursued his passion for coaching football. During many of these years, scraps of paper displaying a series of x's and o's could be found in every corner of our lives. Let me assure you that these had nothing to do with love notes to his honey. I would find them curled up in the washing machine having survived the spin cycle; they would line the night table in our bedroom; and they were stuffed into every jacket pocket. Each one was representative of a brilliant new play for the next practice. Vince Lombardi's autobiography even sat atop my Family History on the coffee table.

I resigned myself to the reality that from the opening kickoff of the Tiger Cat Season in June to the whistle ending the Super Bowl in late January, Joe was deeply ensconced in the world of the gridiron. The worst of it was from Labour Day to whenever his school team, The Brampton Centennial Bucks, finished in late fall.

It had become a tradition that Joe and I would go away each Labour Day weekend. This gave us an opportunity to enjoy the last breath of summer vacation before Joe started back to school. It was also one of the few times we were able to enjoy shopping together. A priority was always to purchase a back-to-school outfit for Joe. He would not only wear these new clothes on the first day of school, but they would also become his official 'game day' wardrobe (all players and coaches traditionally dressed up on the days that football games were played).

On that weekend in 1983, I gently coaxed Joe into buying a pink oxford cloth buttoned down shirt. Our shopping excursion had taken us to Ivy League territory and the preppie look was in all the stores. He originally winced at the idea but remembered that I had rarely steered him wrong regarding his wardrobe. I thought he would look great in this new colour, and while it was a stretch from the mundane beige and blue that filled Joe's closet, I knew he could carry it off.

He wore the new shirt on his first day as planned, with a well-matched tie I had chosen to go with it (my flair for coordinating shirts and ties had begun in the Men's Department at Simpson's in 1968). When he returned home, he had lots to say about the reaction he had gotten from his friends. He had been teased about being a throwback to the fifties and about how the shirt matched the seat covers in one guy's old Chevy. Some even made comments about his sexual preference. The more razzing Joe endured, the more he was convinced he had made the right purchase.

The 1983 football season began the next day. Although anxious to get going, Joe and the other coaches were apprehensive about what they might expect. The previous year had been a wipeout with only sixteen boys making up the team. Most were required to play both offense and defense and they lost every game. They bore the brunt of harsh criticism and cheap comments but played out the season nonetheless. Teachers, parents, even administration questioned the rationale behind them even entering a team in the league this year. Why bother? It's not worth it! Someone's going to get hurt! The coaching staff ignored the concerns, confident that this year would be different.

To the coaches' delight, thirty-two young men registered to play. The committed players from the year before had done an excellent sales job on their buddies, rallying enough of them to enter a full sized team.

Game day was set and Joe wore his pink shirt, much to the chagrin of his co-coaches. On the heels of the previous season's losing streak of ten games, they registered a decisive victory in their first game with a score of 28-0. Teasingly, I suggested to Joe that it must have been the shirt. Game two was another success, followed by a win again in game three. By this time, Joe was pretty certain I was right. The other coaches soon caught the spirit and mustered the courage to purchase their own pink shirts. After their fourth straight victory, players jumped on the Pink Parade.

Think Pink soon became the team's mantra as they started to believe in its power. Prior to their sixth game, they held an assembly to stir up school support. Pink streamers filled the auditorium. Adding to the fun, key players showed up in pink dresses. The student body was now breathing pink air. That day they beat their chief rivals for the second time that season. By this time, word had spread throughout the Board of Education about this raging epidemic. Other coaches knew it could be trouble as they watched this group of designated 'losers' successfully bulldoze the other teams.

On my end, I stayed up late making Power of Pink buttons for the athletic council to sell. At the hospital where I worked, a prominent member of the community had passed away and we were left with a room full of flowers. I chose thirty-six pink carnations and had them delivered to the school for the team to wear during the day of the semi-final game, when, after seven consecutive wins, the Bucks would play a team they hadn't yet met that season.

To set the mood for this important game, a group of students snuck onto the field the night before and painted the goalposts pink. Despite the tremendous crowd support, the Bucks were down 20-0 at half time. Ouch. As the spouse of the coach, I knew what this would mean. Not only would they all be heartbroken, but Joe would also wear the effects of the loss for weeks to come. I was used to the routine.

I could hardly stand to watch this newly high-spirited team

suffer at the hands of the bulk from the other side. During the break, my dad and I left to get a coffee and we purposely took our time returning, in hopes of avoiding further pain. By the time we got back to our seats, just two minutes into the second half, the Bucks had already scored and had possession of the ball again. I couldn't believe it. I had to wonder what words of inspiration had dripped from my husband's frothing mouth in the locker room. (It was probably something along the lines of, "You men will remember this game the rest of your lives ... I want you to leave it all on the field!") By the end of regulation time, the score was 20-20.

The fans electrified the stands. I stood frozen with delight on the sidelines, watching the players pumped to perish their opponents.

Into overtime, the Bucks scored first with a field goal, making the score 23-20. The other team responded with a touchdown. The following point was blocked by the Bucks, so the scoreboard flashed 26-23 for the visitors. Everyone was now on their feet screaming Power of Pink! Power of Pink! Power of Pink!

I followed the play from the sidelines, clutching my own pink fuzzy dice in my jacket pocket. With the minute flag waving and the Bucks down to two plays, the quarterback dropped back and threw an off balance 35 yard pass to a receiver who was not yet there. With desperation in his stride, he dove into the air, arms stretched out before him. As the ball landed in his grasp, he dropped to the ground, bouncing face first into the end zone. As the roar from the stands resonated through the air, the whistle blew to end the game.

It was an unbelievably well orchestrated finish and the fans showed their appreciation. Joe was elated with the victory. As I choked back my emotion, I watched the team collapse into a mound of writhing pleasure.

The Bucks lost their next game to the team that would go on to win the Peel Championship. But it didn't really matter. They were undefeated in league play. They had scored over 170 points and allowed less than 40 to be scored against them. And they had defeated their traditional rivals not once, but twice in the season. What the team experienced that year was a feeling they would not soon forget. They knew they had been a part of something magical.

The Football Team page in the 1983 yearbook appeared as a pink centerfold. To this day, I am certain that anyone who was around the school in the early eighties will remember the year they all went crazy for Pink.

The Unveiling

When I was growing up, I was made to go to way too many Italian weddings. Somehow their importance was lost on me, a young girl more interested in playing baseball with the boys than wearing yet another new frilly dress. Within our extended family, however, there was nothing that compared to the preparation, anticipation and execution of the 'best wedding ever', and like it or not, I had to participate.

As part of the lead-up, there were numerous Sunday afternoon showers to attend (thus earning them a spot on my Top Ten Least Favourite Things To Do list). Consequently, most Saturdays were spent unwillingly visiting fabric stores and searching pattern books to find a suitable dress for my mother, Ida, to make for me. Invariably we would disagree about what I should wear and unfortunately she won out every time.

To prolong the torture, I would also be dragged along for the fabric and pattern selection for the array of other dresses my mom would be responsible for making … for my grandmother, aunts, sister and cousins. If you looked inside my mom's handbag at most weddings, you would not find the usual compact and lipstick but rather the entire collection of spools of thread for each of the dresses that were being worn that day. She liked to be prepared in case a hem came down or button popped.

The weddings back then generally ate up an entire weekend.

The wedding Mass would be celebrated mid-morning and was followed by a lunch. We enjoyed a brief respite mid afternoon, then gathered back at the hall (in yet another outfit, of course) for a twenty-two-course meal. Okay, I'm exaggerating, but only slightly.

During the rest of the evening, I did what I liked doing best: sitting on the sidelines and watching. I'd perch myself on the edge of the dance floor to get a better view of the antics around me. My older aunts dancing together; my uncle and cousin representing the family in dancing the 'tarantella'; and that one couple who displayed the artistry of Fred and Ginger as they swirled and whirled around the church basement floor. I usually fell asleep, sprawled across a few chairs, waiting to go home.

The day after the wedding involved Mass in the morning followed by the inevitable gathering at the home of the parents-of-the-bride in the afternoon for the post mortem. It was there that the real reviews took place.

"Oh, she looked lovely, but that hat her cousin wore? I wouldn't wear it to a dog show."

"I'm so happy she caught the bouquet. Who knows, maybe it will be her time next summer."

"Geez, I was surprised to see how much weight she's gained."

And invariably, "I hope they made good money" (referring to the customary envelopes stuffed with cash and cheques).

When I think back to those weddings now they sound like a lot of fun, but at the time I longed to spend those best weekends of summer anywhere but. So it wasn't surprising that when Joe and I announced our engagement, a part of me was not looking forward to the wedding and all that it would entail. Truthfully, a sense of dread came over me.

The worst part was the anticipation of The Dress. I knew that my idea of the perfect dress would in no way meet Ida's expectations. And it didn't help knowing that whatever dress I purchased would have to be custom made to fit my body. Being extra tall always meant paying extra money.

I took a deep breath and prepared myself for the torment, which started with visits to a myriad of bridal boutiques where I endured the trying on of hideous, ill-fitting masses of billowing white fabric. A typical interchange between us would be:

"I will NOT be seen wearing this."

"Oh, it's lovely. You look so beautiful."

"Ma, I don't care how beautiful I look, I won't be wearing anything remotely close to this."

"Well you don't have any taste at all. This is what all the brides are wearing. It's all the go this season."

She may have been able to bulldoze me as a child, but I was determined to wear what I wanted to my own wedding. With every selection I got more depressed, but the arduous process ultimately helped me come up with a vision of my perfect dress. It would have to be custom made. Although I should have been grateful to have a skilled seamstress at my disposal, oh how I dreaded what would predictably unfold between us. It would be more than the fabric.

My mother agreed to accept the challenge after a mercifully short show of resistance. We started our visits to the fabric stores, scouring every available pattern book. For every vision I had, my mother had an opinion.

"I like this one."

"Oh Carole, you don't like that."

"Yes, I do."

"Fine, do what you want. I don't care."

Which was her ultimate weapon, the tried and true path to victory, the kiss of death to my wishes. It was painful.

With the date approaching and me almost in panic mode, I decided that The Dress would require the blending of three different patterns. My only restrictions on fabric were that it not be too fancy, itchy or clingy. With one month to spare, we had secured the fabric and patterns and the fittings began. With each one, memories from my childhood would fill my brain ... the twitching beneath the fabric, the pins poking into my skin, and the requests to "please just stand still," as my mother did her best to fit me. It was not something either of us had ever enjoyed. But there we were, ready to clean the slate of the past and start again.

As I stood in the kitchen staring out the window, I urged my body to be still. My mother would do her best to place the pins, all the while assuring me she knew just what had to be done to make it fit right. During each of these fittings, the conversation would inevitably include an argument about accessories ... what shoes I would wear, how long the train would be and what about the veil. And every single time the train and veil were mentioned I adamantly insisted that I was not interested in either. I would not, under any circumstances, tote a lengthy train or wear a veil. Was it the reminder of the visions of nuns' habits haunting me, or perhaps the fact that I had seen far too many brides being overtaken by a trailing headpiece and extensive waste of fabric that contributed to my abhorrence of the image of me wearing this traditional bridal garb? Whatever the reason, I was determined not to succumb.

With just five days to spare, and during one of the last fittings, Ida had me standing on a chair in the living room where there was more light. It was time to do the hemline. She had purposely left the fabric uncut, hoping I might change my mind about the train. Towering eight feet over her as she kneeled in front of the chair with her mouth full of pins, I sighed one last time as she appealed to me with questioning eyes.

"No train." I was heartless, but resolved.

She pinned the desired length, then started to sob.

"At least one of my daughters did it the proper way. I don't know why you always have to be different. I just don't understand."

Oh, my God. I could not bear looking down on her like that. I felt like she was Cinderella and I was the wicked stepsister. As much as I was determined to remain firm on my decision, I was wracked with guilt. It didn't help matters that I was aware of the flack my mother was already enduring from the various relatives about the fact that my wedding ceremony had to be held, not in the church, where all true Catholic marriages took place, but out on the shuffleboard in her backyard.

Through her tears, and playing knowingly to her advantage, she made her final move. "But you will wear a veil won't you?"

NO WAY (was what I wanted to say for the seven hundredth time).

"Fine, but only for the ceremony," was what grudgingly came out from between my clenched teeth.

The day before the wedding, I went over to the nearby mall and visited one single store. I asked where the bridal veils were. As the salesclerk escorted me to the section, I announced what the restrictions were ... short, simple and undetectable when looking at me from the front. Within minutes and without trying it on, the job was done and fifteen dollars spent.

Arriving home, I announced that I had bought the freaking veil and as promised would wear it only for the brief ceremony. My mother obviously wasn't happy but chose not to respond, settling for a few subtle bosom-heaving sighs instead.

The wedding day arrived and after a heavy downpour the sun came out and all was set for the short outdoor ceremony. With my back to the guests, I could only assume that my mother was happy because I looked lovely in the beautiful dress she had created for me. And I was wearing a veil.

Time for pictures. As my hand went up to snatch the veil from my head, my mother grabbed it and pleaded, "Just for the pictures."

Fine, but I was NOT happy. So much so that in the first few pictures I was not even smiling.

As we entered the limo to drive to the reception she implored once again, "Please just wear it for the receiving line." Acquiescing once again to her request, but not prepared to be gracious about it, I mumbled my annoyance during most of the ride.

After the last guest came through the receiving line, and as we approached the head table, I did my best to avoid Ida's eye. But like a moth drawn to light, I couldn't help myself.

"Please, just wait until after dinner." I couldn't actually hear the words, but the meaning behind her moving lips was clear. So, in spite of myself once more, I did it.

As soon as the dinner was over, I yanked that thing off my head so fast they might have thought I was going to throw the veil into the crowd of waiting girls instead of the bouquet. By this time I had gotten smart; I just avoided Ida's eye.

I have no idea where that veil ended up after that night (nor do I care) but the twenty-dollar shoes landed back in the box, destined to be returned to the store because the elastic had ripped while I was dancing.

To hear my mother recount the tale of my wedding, you would think I had been the cause of her worst heartbreak ever. Not only did her daughter not get married in a church, she refused the formal photography, had no train and no veil to speak of, turned down the traditional bonbonnieri (Italian wedding souvenirs ... I might have made up the spelling) and opted for a simple, single-tiered cake instead of the customary elaborate concoction.

Her final weary comment was not a new one for me. "Oh, her. I don't know why she just can't try to be normal."

To this day, my mother and I continue to disagree on what's proper, and sometimes I think she doesn't realize that I have grown up somewhat. Recently, as she was fitting Alena for her grad dress, I heard her say, "Alena, please stand still. You're just like your mother."

No, not much has changed.

I still cringe when a wedding invitation arrives in the mail. As I open it, I wonder what on earth can I dig up to wear and how much is supposed to go in the envelope?

The only part I look forward to is the dancing ... which is usually with my sister or cousin, cheek to cheek, just like our mothers and aunts did all those years ago.

Labour Day Weekend

No one can prepare you for childbirth. Doesn't matter how many women insist on sharing their horrendous tales with you, a small part of you believes that your experience will unfold without incident. There are so many things to think about as you prepare yourself for what has been touted as 'the most exhilarating adventure of your life'. The women who believe this obviously were not conscious during childbirth or they have short memories.

First, there is that feeling of having to be in control at all times. As a control fanatic, I figured this would be easy but after a while, you just have to let it go. You want to drink the whole bottle of wine as you smoke that cigarette while horseback riding to Tim Horton's for a coffee after stopping for a whirlpool and sauna at the gym. Yep, by the time I broke my water I was ready. I was ready because I was tired ... tired of strangers patting my belly only slightly above my private parts ... tired of telling people how many pounds I had gained as I stood there looking like *King Kong Bundy* ... tired of imagining what it could possibly feel like to pass that watermelon through what in the past seemed like a very small opening.

Even the thought of breaking my water disturbed me because over the nine months I had been retaining what felt like enough water to wash the driveway, so I was not looking forward to the cleanup without a Powervac. But it did finally happen. Eleven days after my due date, unceremoniously at one o'clock in the morning, the Friday before Labour Day 1985 (with heavy emphasis on Labour). After checking in with my family physician, he assured me that I had indeed broken my water and instructed me to report to the local hospital right away. Having had my bag packed for six weeks (the doctor was prepared to bet his practice I was going to be a month early), I checked in and was told that a specialist would soon be in to examine me and deliver the baby.

As I waited, wiped 'n whined, the time did not pass quickly enough. After what seemed to be the entire staff of labour and delivery including cleaning staff and every available intern coming in to take a peek and a give a touch, the specialist finally appeared. He quickly and without emotion applied the 'finger test'. Then, he patted my leg and promised, "I'll be back!"

What followed were hours of pacing, panting and promising Joe he would not lay his hands on me ever again. Nursing staff who had been in and out all day finally said goodbye and left at the end of their shift. New staff arrived and the routines continued. I had drained myself of all bodily moisture and was only consoled by imagining how much weight I must have lost.

The night passed and by dawn I had clocked thirty-two hours without eating or sleeping. So it meant a new day, a new shift and surprisingly, a new specialist on call (the other one never had come back as promised). His fresh face appeared at the foot of my bed; he announced that my baby should have been delivered the previous day and that we had to get this procedure in gear in a hurry. After his own version of the 'finger test' was applied, he stepped back and looked me over.

"By the way, Carole, what size are your feet?"

My humour quotient and tolerance level being somewhat weakened by then, I snapped back: "Size eleven, what's it to ya?"

Pleased with my answer, he replied enthusiastically, "That's great. I'm only asking because the size of a woman's feet is directly related to the size of her pelvic area and ease of child-birth."

I'm now thinking that this is good news. There is nothing more to worry about, because all I have to do is clear my throat and this kid will slide right out!

It didn't exactly happen that way. By late evening, panic seemed to be reflected in the eyes of the staff (now I know why they wear those masks: to cover up the emotions they wear on their face). The baby was going to have to be taken out soon before danger of a dry birth set in. The physician finally returned from his trip home, during which he had showered, enjoyed an evening out with friends and supposedly waited to be called back for the delivery. He announced his plans to me.

He would try to use forceps, but if they did not work, he would have to do a Caesarian. Hmmm, I thought, forceps … hot dog tongs … I can handle this.

"I can handle forceps, just get the baby out."

But my cockiness was quickly silenced. Instead of the cute little hot dog tongs I had prepared myself for, out came a set of thirty-six inch long blades. The doctor and nurse deemed it a job for two as he took one arm of the forceps and she the other. My left leg was unceremoniously spread open to inject the left blade. The nurse took the other leg, spread it in the opposite direction, and inserted the other blade. In my complete state of delirium, having been 'epiduraled' to my ears, I looked down at my spread-eagled position and asked, "What do you plan to do now? Make a wish?"

The doctor stopped what he was doing; the nurse followed. The tension they had been wearing on their faces slowly seemed to soften as they looked at me and chuckled. He announced to the room of gigglers, "Now that was a good line!"

I believe I saved myself at that moment. Tension was high, fear had set in and exhaustion was extreme; not to mention that I was starving and dehydrated. They were the longest and most draining forty-two hours of my life. But I finally did give birth to a healthy boy.

I remember wondering as I watched my husband sob what the big deal was (the epidural had clearly gone directly to my head). I immediately slurped back a pineapple milkshake and crashed.

I have since heard that we lose brain cells with childbirth ... well, I obviously lost my memory too, because I was back on that same delivery table less than two years later.

"It'll Be Dark There"

When I was growing up I was as obsessed and concerned about how I looked and dressed as anyone else. In the 60's there was little else to grab our attention other than playing our 45's and watching *Shindig* and *Hullabaloo* on TV, whenever our dad wasn't watching *Bonanza*. So I spent a lot of time thinking about what to wear and how to pull a look together from a wardrobe that mostly consisted of uniform pieces. It didn't help matters that my body was not an easy one to fit.

But whenever I miserably determined there was truly nothing to wear, my mom would always come through. Many times she'd save the day (or evening) by staying up all night sewing to ensure I would have something decent to wear and look as good as the 'next one'. I would then try to work some magic applying what little makeup I had collected from my sister's castoffs and had learned to apply from my friends at school.

Finally deeming myself ready, I would head downstairs to await the ring of the doorbell or the toot of the horn in the driveway. Most often it was not a date, but my friend Paula making her first pickup of the evening, since she was the only one who ever managed to get the car.

But before I went anywhere, I first had to pass by my parents for final inspection.

My mom would stand back as if admiring her handiwork, comment on how nice I looked and then make a few last minute adjustments. The threaded needle was always within reach, typically affixed to her housedress for quick retrieval.

I would then turn to my dad for the final seal of approval. "Well, how do I look?"

He would raise his eyes over his glasses and growl ... "You look fine. It'll be dark there."

Of course I would be disappointed because a young girl looks to her father for adoring words. I might have teasingly given him a swat as though to say how dare you. But somehow I knew the point he was trying to make. It didn't matter how many hours I put into looking my best, no one else there would care. They would be too concerned with their own appearance. No one would actually take the time to look at how my makeup had been applied, notice if the seams of my panty hose were straight or if my belt matched my shoes. Most importantly, the truth was it *would* be dark where we were headed ... after all, how much fun would a dance or a party be with the lights on? And I understood the philosophy he was preaching. You feel good? You think you look good? Perfect. Then go out and have a great time. You don't have to rely on anyone's approval.

Ironically when I returned home my mom would jump up frm her sewing and eagerly inquire, Well, did you have a good time? Did anyone say you looked nice?"

"Yeah Ma."

And as I headed off to bed my voice trailed off behind me, "Oh yeah. When I arrived the band actually stopped playing. All the lights were turned on. Everyone wanted to see how nice I looked!"

We'll Trade You Carole

My trip across Canada and around the coasts of the USA stands out in my mind as a treasured memory. It was 1975 and I did the first leg of the journey with Nancy. The only excuse we had for the trip was that one of our profs needed his car driven to British Columbia from Ontario. Neither of us had ever driven a stick shift but that did not prevent us from shooting up our hands to volunteer. Seeing those five provinces from the Trans Canada Highway was the best geography lesson I ever had. No textbook can do justice to the variety of magnificent land forms encountered along the way, from endless prairie to majestic mountains. The views from our car windows were truly awesome.

Nancy and I enjoyed the six weeks of touring together. It was her last blast of freedom before getting married shortly after she returned home. As for myself, with no job in sight, no romantic ties and no desire to be home, I immediately hooked up with another group after Nancy left to tackle the second leg of the journey, the North American perimeter.

There were five of us travelling in an old VW bus, the kind with the rumbling motor that sat in the back seat and with curtains on the windows.. There were no benches or seats behind the front two, so we sat on the floor with our necks stretched and arched to take in the scenery along the way. If we didn't sleep in the van, our accommodation of choice was the Motel

6 because they could be found at most major cutoffs and a double room really did cost only six dollars a night. Okay, so we had to sneak the other three people in each time. We were proud to admit that we only got caught once.

We did most of the tedious driving at night, leaving the days to tour locally and enjoy the attractions and sights of the west coast. We got used to communicating with truckers as they flashed their lights in code to indicate when they wanted to pass or were prepared to let you in, and to express their thanks for your highway etiquette. Often we'd later meet up with them at a truck stop.

At one such stop, we were sitting in a booth cackling as usual and a young woman dropped by to see what all the fuss was about. She stood chatting with us for a while and it was obvious she enjoyed our company. We learned that she was travelling the same route, planning to eventually land in Florida, which was our destination as well. Over the next two cups of coffee she told us that she was having a problem staying awake at the wheel because she had no one to talk to. Without consultation or hesitation my four friends simultaneously blurted, "You can have Carole. She'll talk to you and she'll certainly keep you awake."

Her eyes lit up at the opportunity for company and she answered, "That would be great. I'll trade my TV for her, since it's sitting in the front seat."

The deal had been sweetened and they were happy. Me, well I grabbed my jacket and climbed into her front seat. No use getting my purse and other stuff since we'd be meeting up again before too long. Without making any definite plans, we agreed to travel convoy-style, and speculated that we would probably pull off somewhere around San Antonio and book into the Motel 6.

We drove together for about three hours, always staying within a few car lengths of each other. I lived up to the promise of talking to keep her awake and learned a lot about her and her life. It became apparent that she really wasn't a very happy person and didn't have much of a family life to return to in Florida.

A while later, both vehicles pulled off for gas and then together we headed back onto the interstate. Then, only about two miles later, my new companion took a quick right off the highway towards another truck stop. I bolted upright and questioned what she was doing. She assured me she just wanted to get a drink.

I was now frozen in fear. The van had not seen us pull off, so my friends had no clue we had stopped yet again. With heavy breathing and adrenalin shooting through me, I suddenly realized I was in a potentially dangerous situation with a person I hardly knew. She took her time inside the diner and the longer she dallied, the more scared I got. I jumped into the driver's seat when I saw her come out.

She looked into the window and said, "It's okay, I'll drive."

I shook my head and revved the engine. The second she closed the passenger door, I sped out of the lot, driving over the first curb in my haste. I was initially too panicked to speak but I finally asked her, "What were you thinking? Why did we pull over without letting the others know?"

"Oh, no reason. It's not a big deal."

I got back onto the interstate and more than exceeded the speed limit as I tried to catch up to the van, which was by then a good ten minutes ahead of us. Weaving between the blinking lights of the trucks, I finally saw the back end of the van. Flashing my high beams, I managed to get them to pull over. When we all got out, I said tersely, "I think it's best if I come back."

They looked at each other as if disappointed and JJ finally said, "Ah, do you have to? That means we have to give the TV back."

Safely back in the van, it was clear to me they had no idea that I had temporarily gone missing. I told them my tale emphasizing that the woman was possibly a mass murderer and that I most likely was to be her next victim. And that I had no ID so I would have been unidentifiable. And how scared I was and that I actually was missing them desperately. And wouldn't they have felt guilty knowing that they had so willingly traded me for a TV?

It was dark in the van. I'm sure they just rolled their eyes. In the silence I heard their thoughts whisper, "Hmm, probably not."

Tap Dance Trauma

By the second Christmas of our marriage, Joe and I had decided to set our own standards for gift giving. No more going out and buying a variety of trinkets we'd never use. No more purchasing expensive clothes that we'd never wear and definitely no more impulse purchases that would only prompt the question, "Why would you ever get me this?" The proposal was that we would each determine a theme for the other, which we would keep secret until the moment of presentation. Staying faithful to the chosen theme, we were required to be as resourceful as possible and spend less than fifty dollars.

In the inaugural year of this tradition, Joe's gift set a very high precedent for the many Christmases to come. For as long as Joe had known me, I had been partial to performing a simple dance routine. A tap dance routine. A routine that I executed to perfection on any kitchen tile floor, elevator platform or hardwood hallway. It was comprised of a simple combination of four steps that I had safely kept in the hallowed back room of my memory. As I went through the steps, I would grip an imaginary feather duster in my hand and whisk my path clear in front.

Joe knew the story behind my little performance. I had taken ballet as a child. At the time of the recital, I was chosen to pose as a tree (who stands still in ballet?) while my sister and best friend Teresa delighted the audience with their delicate movements across the stage as flowers.

I quit ballet, believing that tap dancing just had to be more fun. I loved the sound of the clunking and tapping. I wore my shoes constantly and practised every day on the concrete floor in our unfinished basement. I seemed to lose myself in the shuffle step and heel-ball chains. My goal was to progress to the point where I could perform on the upstairs kitchen linoleum. My parents were only interested in seeing the end result of the practising, none of the fumbling around stuff.

It was the Christmas of 1981, and Joe decided that he just had to go with a tap dancing theme for me. He knew he had the right ingredients for a fabulous package, and threw himself into the process of putting it together. Gift #1 was a feather duster. Gift #2 was my old pair of penny loafers made over with a set of taps on each sole. Gift #3 was a certificate for five tap lessons at a local dance studio. I was so excited I cried. This was the best Christmas gift I had been given since I was six, when I received a life sized 'three year old doll', which I still have today.

The lessons started the first Thursday in January. I was so anxious that I decided to drop by the studio earlier in the week just to make sure I was prepared. I approached the young woman at the desk. After I introduced myself and explained the reason for my visit, she laughed aloud and called her co-worker over. Pointing at me she said, "Look, she's the one the certificate was for!"

What was so funny? Did I not look to capable of participating in these classes?

Without letting me in on the joke, she provided the information I needed and then asked, "Do you have the shoes?"

"Ah, yes I've got my loafers."

An expression that looked more like a sneer than a smile appeared on her face. "Do you have a body suit and leotards?"

Remembering the wardrobe I had planned in my mind, I nodded yes.

"Well, that's all you will need. Just show up here around

6:45 and you can change in the room to the left."

I couldn't wait. As soon as I got home I packed my bag. I tossed in the loafers. I rummaged through my old things and found my black polyester bodysuit. I spent ten minutes picking off the matted balls that had formed over the years. Next, I waded through my panty hose drawer and found a pair of black ones that were free of runs and nail polish markings. I tried them on to make sure the band sat at my waist, not under it (low-rise garments were still a thing of the distant future) and that the crotch hung only slightly below the designated area and not just above my knees. It has been a lifelong challenge to find pantyhose that fit my 5'11" frame.

Perfect. I was set. Thursday couldn't come soon enough.

I arrived early to allow for the wardrobe prep and went directly to the change room. I was glad that no one else was around yet because I have never been quite comfortable with open-concept changing. Pleased with the privacy, I felt no urge to rush. I removed all of my clothing and wiggled into my pantyhose. I gave a good tug to get that trampoline crotch up to where it needed to be. I then pulled on the bodysuit. I poked my belly a few times and made sure all body parts were covered. I turned to check myself out in the mirror and was somewhat dismayed to discover that apparently black isn't always as slimming as I was raised to believe.

I then noticed that my bra straps were sitting outside the lines of decency. I tried sliding them back beneath the suit, but it was apparent that the bra had to go. Looking down, I noticed that my underwear was also showing. Not a pretty sight as it billowed unceremoniously out from the bottom of my suit. Clearly, they too had to be done away with. All of this could only be accomplished by undressing completely. I started to panic, because the last thing I wanted was to get caught ... naked that is. I would be mortified.

It was not easy maneuvering all that tight clothing in a rush, but I finally made it back into the pantyhose and body suit and was anxious to see the improvements. I moved right up to the mirror. What a hideous sight: my boobs drooped like beagle ears, stopping just short of the small mound of jelly comprising my waist. I pulled my head up to create more length. I sucked in and tried various postures in an effort to lift the boobs to attention. It was an exercise in futility, and I finally had to accept that I was as ready as I was ever going to be. I put a smile on my face and left the change room.

I stepped into what was now a crowded lobby. The other dancers had gathered in little groups and the room was buzzing with conversation. Some of them were confident enough that they were changing right there in the open. Wow, how liberating would that be? Others had removed their coats, revealing their outfits. I stared in disbelief at the kaleidoscope of colours. They wore fuchsia tights, turquoise suits, hot pink mohair sweaters tied at the midriff. Their shoes were purple, silver or gold; some had bows on the toes. Their hair (they all had big hair) was tied with a bandana or adorned with feathers. Belts sat neatly at their petite waistlines. Their bodies were taut and they carried themselves with poise and elegance. And they were all sixteen years old. I felt like a dinosaur in the midst of a pack of gazelles.

As I scoured the room for a comfortable corner to wait and hide, I felt the eyes of all these young women on me. Many had stopped what they were doing and were checking me out. Some snickered. Some whispered to their friends and giggled. My body drooped lower with every glimpse and I was suddenly hurled right back to that ballet class from twenty years ago. I still did not belong. Resisting once again the urge to bolt, I reminded myself that Joe had bought me a wonderful gift and that I was not here to audition for Fame, just to have fun. Isn't that what all the moms tell their kids? It wasn't 1960, and I could strut my stuff if I wanted to.

I went to all five lessons and added five more for good measure. I did have fun, and when the lessons were completed I finally performed, to a standing ovation, for my parents in their kitchen.

Whoa Wintario

Part of my job at the Mississauga Hospital in 1983 was to plan an entire slate of activities to celebrate the twenty-fifth anniversary of its opening. I loved all the challenges and opportunities to be creative that this task presented. Every day was busy; ideas had to be dreamed up, plans executed, committees rallied, artifacts collected and a schedule of events packaged to attract all sectors of the hospital's extended family.

At the time, the Wintario Corporation held live coverage of each week's lottery number selection at different locations throughout Ontario. In an effort to be as resourceful as possible and to come up with events that would make the celebrations memorable, I looked into the possibility of the hospital hosting the Wintario event during its anniversary week. Little did I realize how much effort would be required to make bright little ideas like this happen.

Back and forth went the communication between Wintario and the hospital. I filled out forms, participated in telephone interviews and submitted every aspect of our organization's plans for hosting the show to the scrutiny of the Wintario organizers. After many weeks of tedious and detailed interchange, we received word that we had passed Wintario's test. Phew! I was proud of my success and excited to participate.

The event was scheduled to take place in the theatre auditorium at Cawthra Park High School on Friday, May 6, 1983.

Some of our responsibilities as host site were to handle all advertising and ticket sales for the event and provide bodies to manage the evening's proceedings. We also had to provide film footage about the hospital to be used as fillers during the half hour TV show and which would serve as promos for us. Some brief interviews with key personnel would also be included.

All of this amounted to quite a commitment of time and energy. The added bonus was that someone had to be designated to 'spin the wheel', the culminating moment of the TV show. Without hesitation, the president appointed me to be the one to cap things off that evening. I guess he figured it would serve as a reward for the months of overtime I had worked ... with pleasure.

Well, as it turned out it was just one more thing for me to worry about. I was directed to look presentable, adhering to very specific guidelines about what not to wear, including stripes, whites and pants, which, other than black, was pretty much all that I had in my closet. What a chore. Pawing through my limited wardrobe, I settled on a navy skirt and a shimmering shirt that had passed the 'Colours' test.

We had a practice run for the evening. My instructions were simple: DON'T SAY ANYTHING and spin the wheel when asked. Hmmmm, the biggest challenge for me was clearly going to be the former. I nervously waited on the sidelines behind the curtain for the signal. There were three hundred people in the audience and hundreds of thousands watching at home, each of them hoping fervently to see their numbers come up when the wheel was spun. Those of you who weren't around during the Wintario years wouldn't know that this show generated the same kind of excitement as one of today's reality shows might.

Bright lights blurred my vision. The emcee invited me out from behind the curtain, introduced me and motioned for me to take my spot on the designated X next to the wheel. There I waited. I looked out at the sea of faces with the words DO NOT SAY ANYTHING ringing in my head. An added self-imposed instruction accompanied them: DON'T DO ANY-THING TO DRAW ATTENTION TO YOURSELF.

Sometimes I get nervous when constraints are placed on my natural behaviour and the way I generally handle this is to smile. Unfortunately, the smile is usually just an early stop along the route to an all out belly laugh. And I was feeling an outburst coming on.

To curtail the sequence, I grinned with my teeth clenched and my lips curled inward. I held this position for what seemed like a very long time. The longer I strived to be still, the harder it got. I saw many familiar faces in the audience, each of whom was waving frantically, making faces and just doing whatever they could to get my attention. However, knowing that my mom was watching and expecting me to 'act proper', I was determined not to deviate from the plan. I figured she deserved that much. Besides, I wanted to see if it was possible to triumph over my inner devilish demons.

Finally, I heard the words.

"Now ladies and gentlemen, the moment we have been waiting for. Will you be Ontario's next millionaire? Let's see who Carole Bertuzzi Luciani will spin for tonight. "Carole, please spin the wheel."

Funny, but with all the details that were covered about the evening, the interminable rules that were issued, the warnings given, the precautions of a practice run taken, not once was any instruction given on the actual spinning of the wheel. Guess I was on my own with this one.

On the emcee's cue I turned towards the wheel and with the physical power I had worked a lifetime to achieve I SPUN the wheel. After the fifth rotation, it was obvious that I had spun it too hard. Around and around it went. After what must have been the fourteenth turn, the emcee interrupted the trance-like state that the spinning wheel had put us all in and said, "Well, Carole, you certainly put a lot of oomph into that spin. We're not used to so much energy."

Knowing I couldn't say anything, I just kept smiling, stared at the wheel and awkwardly waited for it to stop. Just short of the commercial break, the exhausted wheel finally sputtered to a stop, and the emcee quickly announced the winning numbers. I dutifully continued to hold my position, silently choking back all the things I wanted to say to lighten up the situation and introduce some fun into the dreary proceedings. But no, there I stood like an usher in a church: mute, silent and still. I'm sure my friends wondered what the hell was wrong with me.

While the general viewing public would have found nothing remarkable about that evening's broadcast (except those who were lucky enough to have their numbers called, of course), those who knew me and had been forced to watch the torture had a lot to say about my performance after the show. They had been highly entertained by my pained participation and had a grand time making fun of my wheel spinning skills. Happy to have been a source of entertainment in spite of it all, I still wished that I could have let loose. Now THAT would have been memorable.

Think Twice

Why do we sometimes create problems at times when we need them least.

June of 1987 was a particularly stressful time for Joe and me. I had just reluctantly retired from the best job I ever had (other than maybe when I was a camp counselor at Camp Tawingo) at the Mississauga Hospital, and given birth to my second child. In a move that can only be explained by the hormones that were still dancing circles around my good sense, I decided it would also be the perfect time to renovate our very crowded bungalow. Since Joe's job in education allowed him to enjoy a summer free from anxiety, I felt he could easily work alongside whomever we hired to work on the house. To make things even better, we could all move in with my parents. Yes, it was one of those 'good ideas at the time' that looks more like lunacy in retrospect.

By July, we had all but completed the move to my parents' home with the two kids (ages twenty-one months and one month) and workers had been hired. Joe made himself available on site each day, both to oversee the work and contribute his muscle power as needed. And I, the sergeant major, would arrive around quitting time to assess the progress of the day. Pointing to a wall that had come tumbling down, and eyeing the inevitable array of empty Tim Horton cups that were strewn around, one of my typical greetings was, "Joe! Is this all you've done?"

Easily detecting the commando tones in my voice, Joe would reply, "Yeah! You think you could do better Carole?"

Well, that's all I needed to hear. With hand on hip and pointer finger extended, I mercilessly volleyed back, "Joe, depending on where I am in my cycle, I could knock that wall down, put up another, wallpaper and hang the pictures in the amount of time it took you to do this!"

Yep, that was a typical conversation between Joe and me that summer. If we did manage to converse, the loving tones were replaced with mutual snarling. Just the sight of one another could set us off in a round of cantankerous harrumphing. It was becoming increasingly apparent that Joe and I were falling out of 'like' with each other.

Halfway through that gloomy summer, Joe had a great idea. He said, "Carole, how about we go ahead with that vacation we have tentatively planned with that couple we hardly know?"

Before you start imagining us on some exotic island enjoying one another's company again, let me tell you what had been proposed. We would pack up the van with four bicycles and travel to P.E.I., which I believed to be flat, and cycle around it for ten days. This would all be accomplished while my postnatal healing was still in progress, and with acquaintances who only knew us as 'good time Carole and Joe'. We decided to go for it.

The night before we left, Joe thought it would be a good idea for the two of us to go out and talk about the trip. Also on the agenda was to take a stab at thawing out some of the facial freeze that had become a product of all the tension between us.

Off we went to our favourite Chinese restaurant. For most of the date, Joe watched the Jays game on the television mounted in the corner above my right ear, and I, rather than stare into his left ear all night, chose to people watch (i.e. look around and try to figure out who's on a first date, who's having an affair and who's out on the weekly visit with their kids).

As I sat in aggravated silence, it didn't take long for me to think back and fondly recall the courtship days with Joe. How it wouldn't matter where we would go or what we would do; that wherever it was, we would immediately get as close to each other as possible so that we could talk and have physical contact. When we found ourselves in a restaurant in those days, our first goal was to rid the table of anything that separated us, like vases, shakers, menus and condiment bottles so we could zoom in closer to each other. Then we'd talk non-stop, each fixated on the other's face, ignoring everyone else around.

My mind took me back to one such night at the Steak 'n Burger Restaurant in west Hamilton. Joe and I were huddled together as usual when I momentarily came up for air and happened to glance to my right. There sat an older couple. The woman looked wistfully over at me with a wait-'til-you're-married kind of expression on her face. Her companion, looking bored, stared at her blankly and said, "Are ya ready? Let's get the hell out of here. I wanna catch the end of the game."

Chuckling on the inside, I confidently resumed my in-your-face position with Joe and purred, "Joe, look at them. That will never happen to us. Kiss! Kiss!"

But here we were, not seven years later, sitting uncompanionably in our own silence.

Finally, it was time for the fortune cookies. I have my own strategy for reading these. I open one up and if I don't like what it says I tuck it back in. Joe's not too quick. He thinks they come that way. Anyway, I grabbed for the first one and opened it up. Ooh! Obviously it was not meant for me. It read: Think twice before you speak once. I quickly tucked it back in as best I could, just as Joe came to and reached for it. He pulled out the fortune (with great ease thanks to me) and announced, "Ohhh, Carole. This one's got your name on it, Honey."

Not appreciating his sarcasm, I grabbed it and stashed it in my pocket.

The next day we packed everything up, delivered the kids with all of their possessions to the grandparents, secured the house which was still in mid-reno state, and went to retrieve the other couple who anxiously anticipated the start to what they were sure was going to be a highly energizing and entertaining vacation. Little did they know that the relationship between their travel mates had deteriorated into one that was laced with bickering and barking over the summer.

The first eight hours in the car consisted of alternating bursts of negativity and silence between Joe and me. The view from the back seat would have been me looking out the passenger window while Joe leaned towards the left, creating as much space between us as possible. When we arrived in Vermont and checked into the hotel, I was dismayed to learn that I got stuck sharing a room with Joe.

As we unpacked, he said, motioning to the wall that separated us from the other couple, "Carole, we better snap out of this before we ruin our vacation, not to mention theirs."

"Sure Joe, how do you plan to do this?"

Undeterred by my snarky tone, he thought for a moment before saying, "Well, remember the fortune you got the other night with your name on it? How was it worded again?"

"Think twice before you speak once."

"Great … that's it! Tomorrow when we are in the van, (we don't have to start tonight) before we go to say anything, we must rethink it and say it in a positive way."

I thought to myself, how interesting … I'm sleeping with Mr. Positive tonight … but said, "Sure Joe," in the most noncommittal voice I could muster.

Next morning we drove in silence for three hours. My philosophy has always been that if you can't say it the way you mean it, there's no point saying it at all. Eventually, however, I could no longer stand the silence, and besides, I was getting a crick in my neck from looking out the window so long. I faced him. "Jooooooe?"

"Yes Carole?"

"Joe, it could be a lot worse" (always a good place to start).

"Yeah? How do you figure?"

"Well, we could have my mother and the two kids with us."

He nodded appreciatively, so I continued, "Joe, it won't really bother me if it keeps raining for the next ten days like it has been for the past five."

"Why's that Carole?"

"I really like the look of the long dark stripe that goes up the back of cyclist pants on rainy days."

It wasn't that what I was saying was particularly funny, but it was enough of a start for us to realize what was happening. Enough to get us going in a more positive direction. The four of us slowly relaxed; the relief from the couple in the back seat was almost palpable. Joe and I started sharing stories about the horrors of renovation, including building a deck together and wallpapering at three in the morning after the power had gone out. Before we knew it, the energy was back in our voices and our laughter filled the van. It was the spark we needed to take a few good swings at our frustration and allow the dark cloud of doom and gloom to vanish out the open window.

Although our truce didn't make the uphill cycling through PEI any easier, it did ease the tension between us and allowed us to enjoy ourselves, our traveling companions and the experience of the trip we shared.

We have since benefitted repeatedly from the cheap advice stuffed into that fortune cookie. However, the question of just who it was really intended for remains a topic of debate between us.

Shoulder Fashion

$\mathcal{S}$hortly after the birth of Alena in 1990, Joe and I realized it was time for a date. A date that would require me to get out of my sweats and into something halfway decent. I scrounged through my wardrobe, hunting for something fetching to wear, or failing that, something that would fit. The months of hanging unworn in the closet seemed to have altered the shape and size of my clothes considerably. Thank goodness for the elastic-waisted buffet pants that never lost their use or their value.

Reaching into the back corner of the closet, I tugged out a blouse that could have come right out of Linda Evans' wardrobe from *Dynasty*. It was a beautiful shimmering teal blue colour with a slinky satin feel and buttons up the back. I put it on.

Okay, so I couldn't do up the bottom four buttons. It wouldn't be a problem. I looked in the mirror and knew I looked pretty good. I was happy the blouse had shoulder pads, since the fashion experts of the time dictated that all women should wear them. They were the single most important fashion accessory to have in a wardrobe ... padded, sponge-like 'shoulders-to-go'.

Shoulder pads had been very popular in the forties and the current icons of style had sold us on the notion that if worn properly, they would not only make our waists look smaller (the truth ... they just made our shoulders look bigger) but would also enable us to fit into a 'man's world'. The bigger the pads, the greater the power. I had it made.

I looked at myself in the mirror, smoothed the front of the blouse and adjusted the pads. Mmm, mmm, I'd surely be getting Joe's attention tonight. I then recalled reading in J.T. Molloy's book, *Dress for Success*, that if you want to achieve that finishing touch in an outfit, throw on a jacket. Well, I certainly didn't have a jacket that currently fit, so I tried on one of Joe's. I looked in the mirror and adjusted tier two of the shoulder pads. The look wasn't bad.

Realizing there was a wee nip in the air, I decided I'd need a trench coat. Putting one on, things were definitely beginning to bulk up. I looked in the mirror once more and adjusted tier three of the shoulder pads. With my shoulders now somewhere up around my ears and my fingers barely reaching my waist, I studied my image and began to question the thinking behind this look.

Just then, Joe came into the room. He took one look at me and his football coach's eyes lit up. He stared at me through the reflection in the mirror and asked innocently, "Hey, honey. What time's the big game?"

Yep, I had gotten his attention all right.

Medium Black ... No Sugar

Mmmm ... Tim Horton's, the great Canadian equalizer. No matter where you travel in our country, you're sure to find empty Tim Horton's coffee cups guiding your way. One thing you can always count on in this hotbed of caffeine and calories is that there's always something cooking. Not back in the kitchen necessarily, but among the throngs of addicted customers.

I, too, need a Tim Horton's fix most days and my visits usually go without incident. One particular day, however, I found myself waiting in a line-up that stretched halfway into the parking lot. (These ex-policemen really know how to pick a franchise). Not a good start to a day that was chock full of errands. I was experienced enough to know that there wasn't much to be done about it, though, because jumping the line at Tim's is as serious an offence as talking out loud at Bingo ... not something you want to try even once. I knew that there would be no ordering out of turn and that I had better be damn well organized once I got to the front of the line. To arrive there not knowing what I wanted to order would be to risk the pain and humiliation of being loudly singled out for a penalty by the all-powerful server: "Problem customer, possible rookie. Five minutes for stalling!"

I anxiously stood in the cool air of the morning, surrounded by others whose days also could not begin without the customary kick-start. Whenever I take my place in line at Tim Horton's, there is only one thing on my mind. I don't care about the freshness of their doughnuts; I'm not the least bit impressed with their designer uniforms in the unappetizing shade of beige; and being able to eat the flippin' chile bowl does nothing for me. All I want is my 'medium black in a double cup' and the guarantee that when I leave the shop, I will feel no worse than I did when I walked in.

Slowly shuffling my way closer, I finally managed to get inside the shop. Peering from the back and leaning on the door, I counted the heads in front. I then caught a glimpse of the staff working behind the counter. Squinting through the maze, I could see the woman who would be accepting my order. I cringed. With no caffeine in my system yet to help me clear my head, I found myself thinking that she looked like a bulldog. Yes, it was clear to me that she was one of those people who had started to resemble their pet. With her downturned mouth and considerable jowls, she definitely looked like a bulldog. Inching closer, I overheard how she was handling her customers. What a coincidence, maybe it was a stretch, but she even barked like a bulldog.

By the time I got to the glass counter and was able to lean over it to block out the selection of high calorie goodies, I was feeling pretty anxious. I was up next and that meant it was my turn to take some abuse. The Good Humour Angel on my right was whispering, "Come on now, honey, be pleasant. If you try, you can make her day." Battling from the left side, The Mean Spirited Angel (by whom I am most easily and readily influenced), snarled, "Yeah, you can make it more miserable!"

Clearly, the suggestion from the right side was that I do or say something that would turn her wretchedly pinched mouth into a smile, or at least a slight grin. I realized a bit of humour would be necessary, but I needed something to work with. I immediately stepped back to see if there was anything I might be able to comment on. I scanned her with a critical eye, and as I did, my gaze landed on her visor. (Why do they wear those?

In this case it just prevented the sun from improving her disposition). But it wasn't so much the visor that caught my attention as what was sitting right next to the embroidered timbit on it.

As I stared, I felt my pupils enlarge because I couldn't believe what I saw. It was truly a Ripley's Believe It or Not moment. Because there, nestled on her cap, was a plastic pin ... of a BULLDOG! What a bonus. It was too good to be true. I had to go with it. But, again from the angel on the right, a last word of caution was issued: "Honey, if you're going to go for it, I suggest you mumble first."

Good tip. That way if the attempt at humour fails and it doesn't go over so well, you always get a second chance.

So I mumbled, "Is your pin a reflection of your personality?"

With curled mouth and crinkled brow, she snapped back, "What'd you say?"

Phew. I had a second chance. I tried again. Pointing to her pin, I said, "I really like your pin. Where'd you get it?"

With a poke at her visor she growled, "This? The guys over at Mac Truck gave it to me!"

I smirked. I was aware of both the head office nearby and their canine logo.

Prompted by a gleeful pinch from the Mean Spirited Angel, I uttered sotto voce, "They must've pegged you as their mascot."

I may have gotten my medium black that day, but I definitely didn't feel any better when I left. Perhaps I should have asked for sugar.

Carrying the Torch

 $\mathcal{B}$ abe Didrikson was perhaps the greatest woman athlete of all time. She has been my hero since I first read about her in grade five. That year I chose to do my speech on her life. So it's not surprising that I would model my participation in sports after her. My life has been full of athletic activities ever since. However, by the time I was an adult I knew that unlike Babe I would never fulfill the dream to be an Olympian.

The excitement for the 1988 Winter Olympics held in Calgary began in the summer of 1987. Any Canadian could not help but be swept up in it. A major national company sponsored the traditional Olympic Torch Relay, which began in Greece and continued across continents and through each of our ten provinces.

The process for selecting torchbearers was by lottery, and ballots were available at local gas stations. I decided this was something I deeply wanted to do. It would not only be exciting to be a part of this worldwide event, but I could only imagine how much fun it would be. My strategy was to complete one ballot for each leg of the run that was within an hour's drive of my home, and two for those that were within half an hour. In total, I entered my name thirty times.

That summer was incredibly busy with both the birth of our second child and a major renovation to our home. Thoughts of the contest were relegated to the back of my mind. One afternoon in late August as electric saws hummed along with the baby's cries, I searched for a ringing phone. Ah, there it was under the tarp that was meant to prevent all that awful plaster from filtering through my home. Diving for it before the answering machine flipped on, I panted out a harried, "Hello." I'm sure it sounded like a yelp to the person on the other end.

The conversation that followed went like this:

"I would like to speak to Carole Ber-toot-sie Lu-chainy."

"Um. Yes, that's me." Ouch, yet another mispronunciation of my name. It was probably another carpet cleaner looking for my business and I just didn't have time for this interruption.

"Well, I'm calling from The ABC Marketing Company regarding a ballot you submitted for the Olympic Torch Relay."

"Yyyyeeesss!" I didn't want to appear too eager in case it was one of my friends trying to trick me.

"Well your name has been selected ... "

I immediately interjected, "No way. Who is this?"

"Yes. I'm holding your ballot in front of me. Do you live at ... ?"

"Yep. That's definitely me."

"Well, if you can answer a simple skill testing question you will be carrying the torch on December 25th of this year."

"Come on. You're joking, right?" At this point, I couldn't think straight with all the noise in the background and dust in the air, but the slightest possibility that it was legit was making me a little tense.

"No, I'm not and as I said, if you can answer a skill testing question ... "

"Okay. Okay. What is it?" My anxiety was peaking. I needed the question.

"Here's the question: 2 + 4?"

"6."

"6 x 6?"

"24."

"I'm sorry. What was that you said?"

"24."

"Would you like to try it again?"

"Yeah, sure (though I was sure I had not made a mistake). 2 + 4 is 6. 6 x 6 is 24."

"Carole, just take your time. Let's go over it again."

By that point, I had lost my patience. Dante was tugging on my leg. Vincent's wailing had been turned up a notch and the buzz of the saw had been replaced by a sledgehammer to the wall. I was losing my grip.

"Okay. 2 + 4 is 6. And 6 x 6 is 24."

"Now Carole, I would really like you to be able to have this opportunity. Please, just relax and think carefully about the question."

Talking faster, I recited it again. Was she hard of hearing or what? I didn't understand what the problem was. It was grade 3 arithmetic, for Pete's sake.

I repeated my answer, only louder. "2 + 4 is 6. 6 x 6 is 24."

In all my righteous certainty I was about to suggest that she check her calculator, when I spotted my own mini one sitting on the table near the phone. I quickly typed out the numbers. Oh no! How could I be so dense? Childbirth must have obliterated some brain cells. Staring at the red 36 in the window of my calculator, I took a deep breath.

"I think I would like just one more chance. Please understand I am more intelligent than I happen to sound right now. I do have a lot going on that is affecting my concentration. Please bear with me."

"No problem, Carole. Just take your time, I'm rooting for you."

In a calm voice, I recited the newly discovered truth: "6 x 6 is absolutely equal to 36."

She then completed the series of questions, which I managed to answer successfully. She congratulated me (wow, that was painful) and assured me that I would soon receive the details about the relay in the mail.

For the next three months I could not stop thinking about the run. I marveled that I had been chosen to participate in this historic event on Christmas night in Hamilton, the place of my birth and where most of my extended family still lived.

I followed the reports about the relay starting with the kickoff day in mid-November. Excitement escalated as it entered the Toronto area. It was due to pass through Oakville in the early morning of December 24th. I set the alarm.

That morning I bundled up the two kids and headed to the route for the early morning start. Hundreds of people lined Lakeshore Road to witness this great event. A huge breakfast party was taking place downtown. I found myself a spot that afforded the best view. I had one child in a stroller and wore one in a Snuggli on my chest. It was cold and still dark, but I was determined to witness this special event. I waited in great anticipation, realizing that I was about to tip the excitement scale and wondering how I would be able to wait for my own moment of pride.

Finally, I saw the headlights of the safety vehicle heading towards us, and behind it, the flame of the torch soaring in the air. With no regard to the child who was attached to me, I jumped up and down, waving with all my might in hopes of catching the runner's eye and thus 'sharing the flame'. But alas, faster than the Popemobile, the runner sprinted by me with such speed I thought the flame would go out. His face had a look of sheer determination. He gripped that torch like a corporal with a surrender flag. He did not share one spark of that flame with anyone.

To everyone's great disappointment, he did not invite the excited onlookers to celebrate with him in this moment of national pride. Some people yelled out to him, but his gaze could not be diverted. We all headed back to our cars feeling cheated. My own feelings of frustration only fuelled my eagerness to do it right the following night. I was determined that it would be different. No one would go home regretting that they had come.

The next day we celebrated Christmas morning with our two young children, and for the rest of the day I excitedly envisioned what would happen that night. My entire family planned to be at the run, postponing traditional dinner plans until Boxing Day.

Clad in my uniform (and no I would not sell it for anything) I arrived at the designated meeting place in plenty of time. The organizer informed us that each of us would run with the torch for one kilometer. The other runners would follow in a van and when it was our turn, we would jump out to receive the torch from our mate.

As it happened a mix-up occurred, which meant that I would have to run 1.6 kilometers. At that point, I'm sure a marathon would have been a breeze. My feet barely hit the pavement as I began my leg of the run. The smile never left my face and I carried that torch so high, onlookers could have seen it a mile away. I was determined to share the flame with as many people as possible. I zigzagged across the four-lane street. I stopped to let people touch it, and to pose for photos with it. When I reached the four way stop of a major intersection I ran a 360-degree route around. Some people ran alongside me to 'catch the spirit' up close. By the time I reached my family, the cameras were clicking furiously to capture this moment in our history forever.

Nearing the end of my route, the escort runner sidled up to me and said, "You're really enjoying this aren't you?"

My simple response was, "I sure am. I will never have this opportunity again, so I'm going to milk it for all it's worth."

At the ceremony later that night, we had a more intimate celebration with other torch runners and our families. We were all awarded a special certificate embossed with the Olympic Seal. To our amazement, it officially recognized each of us as a participant in the 1988 Winter Olympics.

I couldn't help but think of Babe.

a: reunion

It was the time to meet and plan a special fortieth birthday reunion for our classmates from St. Joe's. We hadn't had a reunion since graduation in 1972. A few of us who had stayed in contact over the years put together the planning committee. We started meeting eight months before the proposed event to work towards establishing a mailing list to be used for invitations.

Prior to our first meeting we learned that one of our classmates who would be helping out had recently been diagnosed with colon cancer. She had undergone surgery to remove her colon and apparently everything was fine. We were upset by this. We wished we could have known sooner so that we might have been able to support her through it. Away from her, we expressed concern to each other and could only hope that everything was okay. We were also a little anxious about how to approach the subject with our friend when we saw her again.

When we finally met there were lots of hugs all around. Pleasantries were exchanged and sincere good feelings were shared with each other. It was obvious that we were ecstatic to be together again. Our friend's health was not discussed.

We went about the business of tracking down addresses of other classmates. It was tedious but we managed to have enough good laughs to keep us going. After four hours of work we called an end to our efforts for the day. We were all getting a bit giddy anyway.

My friend Paula had been inputting the necessary data into the computer as quickly as we collected it. Before we left, she announced, "Here's the disc with our addresses. The code to the program is a:reunion." (aka: A Colon Reunion)

Quick to the draw, I heard these three words and muttered "Uh, oh!"

Our recovering friend, not missing a beat blurted out, "Oh, no. That means I can't come!"

We laughed until we cried. We hugged each other with relief.

It was what we needed to break the silence. Our friend wasn't alone anymore.

Hard Question, Doc?

When one of my sons (I'll keep it vague so it won't find a spot on Facebook) was eleven months old, I noticed something peculiar. From the moment I first changed his diaper that morning his penis was erect. As a mother I had to wonder what kind of dreams he was having. Each time I changed him that day, the status remained the same. By mid afternoon I was concerned enough to call the doctor. My son was also coughing a lot so I figured the doctor could check out both concerns. I was not one to run to the doctor about every minor sniffle and odd behaviour, but this did worry me.

I was able to drop by the doctor's office the next morning. Twenty-four hours after I first noticed the symptom, it continued to stand at attention. As I sat in the waiting room I tried to prepare myself for the explanation. We were eventually called into his office. We made friendly conversation and then the doctor asked what he could do for me.

I explained about my son's cough, and P.S. "He's had an erection for over twenty-four hours." I tried to drop the words from my mouth as quickly as possible and without animation so as not to create any drama.

The doctor started with the stethoscope to my son's chest. He checked his back. He looked into his ears and throat and then had a good search through his eyes. As he scribbled something on his chart I interjected, "You might want to look at him, to see what I mean." I tried to keep it vague enough that I wouldn't have to use the 'p' word in front of my shy doctor again.

It appeared that he didn't hear me. I continued, "Yes, it was so strange to see it so firm. It made it difficult to fold the diaper over. I was worried about hurting him as it bent forward." Nervousness had kicked in on my part and in the face of my doctor's silence I was getting worried that I'd have to leave without an explanation.

The doctor eventually interrupted me, motioning me outside into the hallway by the waiting room so that he could weigh the baby. I continued my jabbering…"Like, is it normal to be like that for so long? Might he have a problem? How long can this go on?"

He weighed him and we went back into the office. The doctor then handed me a prescription for the cough and stood up. It was clear that he had heard enough and felt it was time for me to go. As I proceeded to leave, I was distressed that he had not yet addressed my concern. There we stood in the hallway, within hearing distance of the growing crowd in the waiting room.

I seized my final chance to speak, "But Doctor, what do I do about his permanent erection?"

He finally answered, "Carole, it's normal. Eventually it will go down."

Feeling relieved, I made my way towards the exit. At that moment I caught the gazes from those people in the waiting room. They looked at me with expressions ranging from curled up grins to wide-open smiles.

I smiled back. I'm sure they thought I was complaining about my husband.

The 10th

I guess you can say Joe and I go the distance to keep the gears of our marriage lubricated. I make it my priority to do as much as I can to keep the interest alive. After all, if I'm going to live the rest of my life with this guy, I might as well make the best of it. To this end, I will use any excuse to employ my creativity to plan something both fun and exciting for the two of us. We all know relationships need special attention, but our fast-paced lives rarely leave the time we need to work on them.

As we approached our tenth anniversary, I dreaded the milestone. Truthfully, I almost always dread our anniversary. It's because of the date on which it falls … June 30th. By this time each year I have usually fallen out of 'like' with Joe. June is perpetually a stressful time in education and Joe seems to carry the weight of the entire year on his face and in his heart. If anything, I usually try to keep my distance during this period.

However, one year my friend Liz successfully goaded me into planning something special. In discussion, we both realized that many couples are hanging onto their relationship by a thread. I confessed that ours was more like a bungee cord, each of us tugging in opposite directions throughout the school year. Inevitably we bounce back to 'home base' for the summer, but for some reason I just didn't feel like making the effort that year. Life on my end of the cord was fine, thank you. But Liz persisted, so I buckled down and put my creative talents to work.

I decided that a twenty-four hour mystery tour would be the best idea, since it would probably take at least half of that time to start being comfortable with each other again.

To get in the mood of our wedding day, the first thing I did was dye my prematurely greying hair back to its original dark brown. I then called Joe's school and left a message for him to meet me at an infamous store that sold adult toys and pleasures.

Rushed, having left a meeting early, he reluctantly showed up at the shop. I encouraged him to pick up a few things that he might enjoy using later in the day. Embarrassed, he went along with my request. For the first time that month he actually looked at me and smiled. He liked the hair! Before he returned to fulfill his last duties at work, I suggested he meet me at home by 3:00.

By the time he arrived back, I was already packed and in the car, ready for the date to begin. Treat number one for him ... I drove! Our first stop was a relaxing game of miniature golf. Okay, so the real reason I picked that activity was because I had a coupon that expired that day, but it turned out to be a fun way to wind down. By the sixth hole, Joe and I were already engaged in our ongoing friendly rivalry.

Golf game completed, I drove the scenic route to Cootes Paradise, a spot Joe and I regularly visited when we were dating. I had prepared a selection of assorted snacks (i.e. leftovers from the shrimp dinner Joe had made the night before). The wine was particularly effective for relaxing Joe as he managed a quick power nap before we continued. Getting into the spontaneity groove, Joe decided to interrupt the tour by having us drop by his old barber to have his beard shaved. He emerged looking just like he had on our wedding day. Next we took a long walk through our old dating area and desperately tried to call up the part of our lives that had been inadvertently packed away in the dust of our memories.

Dinner was reserved for us at the restaurant where our wedding reception had been held. We sure did miss the two hundred and fifty guests from ten years earlier because all of a sudden we found making conversation face-to-face a bit of a challenge.

A movie followed: *Great Balls of Fire*, something nice and light. As we enjoyed an ice cream cone at Stoney Creek Dairy, Joe quizzed me about where we would be staying that night. I simply said, "You'll see."

We left Hamilton and headed east along the QEW. He guessed that we were heading to the airport strip where we spent our wedding night. Nope! He wondered if it was Harbour Castle, where we had enjoyed a brunch earlier in the year. Sorry. He could have guessed forever but would not have come up with the spot I had chosen, thanks to the expert advice of Liz.

The honeymoon suite had been reserved for us at the recently renovated but ever-so-tacky Sea Horse Motel on the sleazy Lakeshore strip in west Toronto. I unloaded my supplies: the goodies purchased earlier in the day, the tape deck and assortment of favourite tunes, small bottles of liqueur, and a special breakfast prepared for the next morning. I had thought of everything.

Without getting too specific or sharing too much, we thoroughly enjoyed the hot red stand-up Jacuzzi that night, and made full use of our earlier purchases. The circular bed provided plenty of play area and we were completely fascinated by the dancing lights around the room. We managed to keep track of one another by regularly checking the strategically placed mirrors both above and around us. We definitely had fun that night.

An early morning run along the lake and then it was time to enjoy our fresh strawberries, champagne and orange juice breakfast. Wow. It was too much for Joe to handle. And it was only 10:00 a.m.

We checked out and waved goodbye to the Seahorse with a chuckle. We hoped no one would recognize our car as we left.

Next stop was a visit to Queen's Quay. We walked through the shops and enjoyed the view of the lake on an absolutely perfect Canada Day. I slowly maneuvered Joe to the dock. There, waiting for us was a gondola, staffed by a pseudo Italian paddler and stocked with a freshly prepared gourmet lunch. Sipping Spumante, we waved to the onlookers on shore and sang Italian songs. On the relaxation scale, Joe was dinging the bell at the top.

Back on shore, we headed up towards the Sky Dome for a whiff of the game day atmosphere. Joe had already mentioned what a perfect day it was for a baseball game. The Jays were playing Boston. We had honeymooned there. I couldn't resist! Tucked away in my pocket were two box seat tickets I had managed to wangle from my brother.

Three hours later, having spent a glorious day watching baseball in the sun, we prepared for the finale. Our date was going to end where our marriage had begun … in my parents' backyard. So before we went into their house to fetch our boys from their overnight visit, we had one more thing to do. Our date would not be complete without a quick pose on the shuffleboard … where we had exchanged our wedding vows ten years earlier.

In an action packed twenty-six hours, Joe and I managed to rekindle the flame that had been reduced to a faint flicker. We were back in 'like' with each other, and our romance had been rebooted. Joe's end-of-school-year tension had been willingly replaced with a grin that screamed satisfaction.

We didn't buy any souvenirs that day to remind us of our very special tenth anniversary. We only took one photo. Not much else was necessary. Nine months later our third child Alena was born, and in the birth announcement I fittingly made honourable mention of the Sea Horse Motel. Appreciating the plug, they sent us a gift certificate for a complimentary night in the honeymoon suite. Unfortunately, they closed down before we were able to cash in. Too bad; I could have used that certificate for our thirtieth wedding anniversary this year.

Rain Dance

Somehow, clear and rational thinking seems to cloud over immediately after childbirth. This must be why Joe and I made the decision that camping would be a great vacation for our family of five just three months after Alena was born. The fun part was that we would be joining three other families of friends, so it would be something of a party. We packed half the contents of our bungalow into our Yuppie minivan. Not being seasoned campers we lacked the essentials that all of our friends had ... elevated campers, portable potties and enough tarps to shelter Wawa. My friend Paula was particularly adept at this as she wrapped the entire campsite in plastic at the slightest hint of rain.

Once we actually found a place for everything and set up home camp we were ready to enjoy three nights in the woods. It was cozy in our tent, which the box had promised would sleep five people comfortably. You know how guys lie about their height? Well, apparently the same applies to tent box promises because roomy it wasn't.

We eventually got the children settled amidst all of our belongings, sleeping bags and baby paraphernalia. The only way we could be comfortable was if we all slept like spoons. If just one of us turned, we either poked the side of the tent or rolled over a child. Alena had the best setup, enjoying lots of room in her playpen, smack dab in the middle of all the chaos. The only way to get the kids settled was if one of us lay in the tent with them. So for that reason we had brought along our boom box (which meant we didn't have to miss a Jays game either). As we fell asleep that night, we promised one another that if things did not work out we would simply pack up and head home.

Sleep was not easy. Conscious of the baby's every move, I bolted up at the slightest whimper and whipped a bottle, soother or her own thumb into her mouth. Anything to be sure she did not wake the camping neighbours an arm's length away. I imagined the warden knocking on the tent handing us our eviction notice.

Tossing and turning all night (in unison, of course), we couldn't help but hear the rain begin. Once it started it did not let up. It rained and rained and rained and just when we thought the sky had finally dried up, it would pour again. With each drop, the air got cooler and we were forced to cuddle closer together. We cursed not having had tarps to hang like our friends. I complained that if only we had bought the bigger tent, there'd be more air flow.

One by one, each child woke up. Time check 6:15 a.m. and everyone was awake and it was still raining. The water slowly began to bubble on the edges of the tent. As we quickly moved everything out of the way, puddles began to form in the corners and the air continued to cool. Staring at the top of the tent where droplets had developed, we quietly wondered how long it would take us to pack up. We began to question our sanity in having even attempted this. We tried to imagine the rest of the day cooped up in here with the three kids. Joe's thoughts were, no doubt, even more somber than mine ... trying to picture the rest of the day cooped up with me in there.

Fortunately, we didn't dwell on these thoughts for too long. Instead, we turned on the radio and happened upon a Motown station. We couldn't believe our good fortune. We love Motown and we love to dance. So as we waited for the rain to lose its power, Joe and I stood up (right smack under the dome) and started to dance. The kids couldn't figure out what was going on. Alena cooed in her playpen. Dante asked, "Mommy, why are you doing that?"

Remembering a popular line from my youth: 'Might as well, can't dance', I responded with the flipside ... "When there's nothing else to do, you might as well dance."

On the way home a few days later I solicited trip evaluations from my kids like I usually did.

"Who had fun? Put up your hands!"

All hands shot up (except for Alena's ... she was sound asleep.)

Like a true recreation coordinator, I wanted to know the specifics.

"What was the most fun?"

You know the answer.

Battle in the Stands

*O*ur family had proudly held season tickets to the Hamilton Tiger Cat football games since 1952. One could say we were die-hard fans, travelling all the way from Mississauga to see the games. It was a ritual we all enjoyed. Our favourite game each year was the Labour Day Classic in which the Ti-Cats faced off against the Toronto Argonauts. The rivalry between these two teams has existed in some form or another since 1876.

In 1989, four of us headed out to see this big game together. The quartet consisted of my dad, who at seventy, saw himself as something of an aging *Rambo*; my brother, a successful labour lawyer; my husband, a high school teacher and football coach and me, pregnant with our third child.

The usual routine started with a brisk walk from the parking spot nicely reserved for us two miles from the stadium (anything to save a buck). Our pace was always too quick for casual conversation as we all focused on the task at hand: to get to Ivor Wynne (now known as I-never-win) Stadium without being run over and in time for the kick-off. Our seats were the best ... fifty-yard line, top row of the north side of the stadium. Getting there required negotiating a narrow stairway with way too many short steps, making it difficult to climb without watching your feet. Since we could only climb in single file, we were led by my dad who, despite his age, was the fittest one in the group and also the most committed to getting us to our seats without missing a 'down'. He led the way in silence, carrying a fold-up metal stadium seat for his aging back. Behind him, chatting the whole way, was my brother Larry, and behind him came Joe, who listened intently to my brother's unsolicited opinions and chatter. Holding on to Joe and pushing from the rear, I waddled along not really caring whether or not I missed the entire first half of the game.

The Labour Day Classic was usually the highlight game of the 'home' schedule. It was guaranteed to supply lots of action both on the field and in the stands and it was one game we never missed. The noise level was loud, spirits were high and the fans were pumped. Pigskin Pete frenetically led us in ever escalating rounds of the 'Oskie-wee-wee' cheer.

From our spot high in the stands I loved to watch the crowd, enjoying the view of their backs as they shouted obscenities and high-fived each other without spilling a drop of beer on souvenir jerseys, that were often strained by expanding bellies. It was always an entertaining crowd.

My dad sat wedged up against a steel pole which supported the east side of the Tim Horton's sign, studying the field with the eyes of a critic, Larry and Joe stood up for the entire game, Larry commentating on the play action and Joe yelling, "C'mon ref, you gotta make that call!"

On this day the stands were full and they were rockin' from the opposing camps of ardent fans. The mass of yellow and black was raucous with their 'Oskie-wee-wee' cheers. The 'Argo-nuts' bellowed out their signature cheer from the end zone ... a deep, loud and extended yawn in the sound of AR-RRRRRGOOOOOOs ... which was invariably snuffed out by a quick rejoinder from the Ti-Cat crowd: "SUCK!"

We had witnessed numerous Ti-Cat losses to the Toronto crew over the years, but on that day they were actually beating 'the brats from the other end of the QEW'. It seemed like a momentous accomplishment, making the long drive, walk and climb worth the effort. With a firm lead in place and five minutes left in the game, my father decided that since his support and guidance was no longer needed it would be smart to leave the packed stadium before the rush. No discussion, we followed.

As we made our way across the top of the bleachers, we noticed an overabundance of drunks wandering around. Although Tiger Cat fans are always good-natured, well-behaved and fun loving, the fans from visiting teams don't always know how to behave. This day there was a group of guys who were obnoxious, loud and arrogant. I guess they just weren't too happy about a potential loss to their rivals.

My dad, brother and husband headed down the stairs along the edge of the stadium, trying to keep a wide berth from the rowdies. I attempted to keep my position, but managed to become separated from them by a pair of young Tiger Cat fans. Swaying together and waving their homemade banner, they chanted, "Tigers ate 'em raw!" Following them and immediately in front of me were three drunken Argo fans decked out in blue denim. Whether it was due to the game's outcome, the over consumption of alcohol, or having had to endure one too many 'Oskie-wee-wees' for the day, this group was not happy. They made it clear that they were looking for some trouble, and at that point I was thankful for my view from the back.

There was a backlog of movement on the steps ... small steps forward, pause, back up and start again. The once orderly line had morphed into a giant blob trying to jam its way down the stairs. It was then that the obstreperous Argo fan decided to push right through the young 'banner wavers', sending my father over a bank of seats. Not knowing what had hit him, my father spouted off a slew of the most colourful words I had ever heard come out of his mouth. Not only was he ticked, but it was obvious he was shaken from the fall. Joe jumped over the seats to get to him. As the only true caregiver amongst us, he made sure that my dad was not hurt and tried to help him up. In keeping with his character, my dad was too proud to be helped and too pissed to be grateful.

My brother, who had seen what had happened, and that

my dad was well enough to be mad, decided to continue down the stairs. Being the typical labour lawyer, he then decided that it would be a good idea to talk about the incident with the drunks.

All four of us found ourselves back on the stairs, following Larry's lead. My father, still spewing and fuming, was convinced that he could take this guy on and was determined to get even. Joe supported him from behind and, in preparation for the potential confrontation, expanded every muscle in his body to the point where he began to resemble *The Incredible Hulk*. Still trailing, I protected my belly and prayed to Saint Jude (patron saint of hopeless cases) that no trouble would follow.

We eventually faced the three drunks at the bottom of the stairs. Larry presented his case: "Now that wasn't too bright, pushing over the young boys and knocking over my father, was it?"

The most belligerent of them replied intelligently, "F--- the old man."

My father, no longer able to restrain himself, took a swing at the guy with his metal seat (see, it protects more than his back), hitting him squarely on the corner of his head. Joe, pumping himself up to even greater proportions, stared the guys down as only men can do when they try to intimidate each other. Impressed as I was by the prowess of my menfolk, all I wanted to do was get the heck outa there before somebody really got hurt.

Thankfully, assistance came before any more damage was done. The troublemakers were escorted away, with their leader still rubbing his head where my dad had cracked him. Larry continued to talk while Joe slowly deflated himself. I picked up my pace as I repeatedly checked over my shoulder, not believing it was truly over until we were safely back in the car.

Every game that followed, my dad never ceased to scan the crowd as he looked for the offending guy. At just the mention of the incident his tough persona reemerged, with lips pressed, fists clenched and head shaking.

I learned a lot that day. Each of us experienced the same situation, yet all of us reacted differently: one wanted to talk about it, one wanted to beat the crap out of the offender, one nonverbally strived to intimidate, and one just wanted to run away.

Labour Day Classic? That's for sure.

Dick

There are days when I question my ability to cope with parenthood. Many days I retreat into my shell, wallowing in self doubt as chaos dances around me. December 1989, too cool and dark to be outside, there I sat overwhelmed on the couch with my two overactive young boys. Dante was freshly four, Vincent was two and a half and I was pregnant with our third. Christmas was more than in the air ... it filled their thoughts and buoyed their spirits. As I moped away that day, I tried to gather the strength to face it all head on.

Deep in thought, I was interrupted by the squeaky sound of Vincent's voice (an early and eloquent talker). In his hands he clutched two figures of Dick Tracy. One was a three inch immobile moulded plastic figure and the other was six inches tall and had movable parts.

He started. "Mommy, it's not fair. Dante's Dick is bigger than mine," aptly displaying the difference before my eyes.

"Look Mommy, his Dick bends and mine doesn't.

Mommy, look how big Dante's Dick is and mine is so small. It's not fair, Mommy. Mine is so little I can hold it in one hand, and you can play with Dante's because it moves ... not mine."

Barely able to squelch my laughter in the face of his distress, I managed to suggest, "Vincie, I think you're gonna have to work something out with Dante. Maybe he will share."

He left to negotiate. He quickly returned and announced excitedly, "It's okay, Mommy. Dante said I could play with his Dick whenever I want as long as I don't break it."

A big smile lit up his little face.

I don't have to explain the effect this scenario had on me. My mood immediately brightened and I was eager to share this juicy nugget of reality. The only hard part would be convincing people that I hadn't made it up.

Hypnotized in Silk

A trip to Bermuda with my parents, aunt and uncle, sister and brother-in-law and Joe was the highlight of the summer of 1980. Each day we enjoyed all of our meals together, lots of early morning tennis and the occasional round of golf. Afternoons were spent lounging at waterside or touring the island on mo-peds. By the evenings we were typically so tired we just wanted to relax in the lounge and be entertained. This element of the trip peaked on the final night when we made a reservation to visit a nightclub in town. The headliner was *The Incredible Reveen ... Hypnotist Extraordinaire.*

The warm-up comic was good but it took Reveen's presence to really electrify the audience of over a thousand. He dazzled us with his photographic memory and he mystified us with his magic. He even intrigued many of us enough to take the stage at his request.

It was the segment of his program in which he would hypnotize willing audience members. To determine this select group, he invited anyone who was willing to try the first round of exercises. Of course I was in. As we listened carefully to the instructions of his silken voice we each did our best to concentrate. Simple. All that was required was to imagine that our hands were stuck together and that the force of a sledgehammer couldn't break them apart. At his gentle touch, only the stubborn subjects progressed to the next round, and in minutes he had whittled the eager crowd of participants down to the chosen dozen. Surprisingly, my frenetically natured self had survived all of the cuts. I had made the team. What I had not yet figured out, though, was what exactly we had been chosen for.

I found myself carefully sizing up my teammates. What had I done? How could I, the one who has difficulty concentrating on anything, be selected? How was it possible that I had managed to focus long enough to earn a spot up on the stage?

Everyone in the group sat like rag dolls. Their eyes appeared to be glazed over. They followed each syllable from Reveen's mouth, nodding in unison like puppy dogs. Surely, I couldn't have become a member of this flock! I looked out at the audience. It was dark and the spotlights obstructed my view. I glanced to where my family sat and saw them waving their arms at me. Except my mother. Her head was down. I knew the look. She was praying that I wouldn't embarrass myself ... or her.

Reveen then asked the audience to applaud for the twelve on stage for we would be their entertainment for the evening. This announcement caused me some anxiety as I wondered what I had gotten myself into. I consoled myself with the thought that at least I looked good in the new off-white raw silk outfit I had just purchased.

For the next three hours, Reveen led us in and out of deep trances. He assured us that we would not do anything against our will; we would not do anything immoral; and we would not have to do anything that might embarrass us. Yeah, but by whose standards?

I sat there half waiting for the next instruction and half shaking my head at the insanity of his suggestions. Yet, each time the pendulum, boomerang or any other trinket he had us imagine would come heading my way, I too lost my senses. We performed in a symphony. I played the trombone. We sang at Carnegie Hall. I belted out my favourite camp song. We starred in the Greatest Circus Show on Earth, spent a day at Disneyland and enjoyed a wavy sail in the ocean where our boat capsized, forcing us to swim to shore. So much for my new silk outfit.

Through each routine, I watched my teammates in amazement. They were hysterical. I couldn't imagine what they were thinking as they gave themselves over to each outrageous command. I truly did not belong there...or so I thought.

By the end of the evening the audience had laughed so hard I'm sure their bellies ached. Reveen then spoke to each of the participants separately. Placing his hands on our shoulders, he granted each of us our lifetime 'souvenir'. For some, it was no longer having a fear of crowds, for others the end of cigarette cravings. My turn. His piercing eyes glared through to the back of my head. His grip tightened on my shoulder (I hoped it wouldn't destroy the shape of my new shoulder pad) and with a jolt he announced I would no longer fear the dentist's chair. I wondered if someone had told him about the many and painful 'teeth dreams' I had endured since I was a child.

One by one we left the stage, only to be stopped in our tracks for one final demonstration of courage. You see, toward the end of the program he very subtly issued each one of us a last instruction for the evening. He then concluded the show by addressing the entire group with this statement: "You will go forth and tell the masses about this great show, thereby guaranteeing sell-out crowds for its duration."

Thinking the show was over, no one paid much attention to the various individual instructions. However, the escapades resumed as we each tried to return to our seats. A few let on they were at a rock concert of their favourite band. They screamed, they waved their arms and they wriggled their bodies to thumping music that no one else heard. Two of us had our feet stuck to the floor and couldn't take our next step. One poor gentleman had suddenly realized he was naked. And the best was at the very end when a woman jumped up and started screaming that the Martians were coming, and that we had better listen carefully to her instructions. She stood on a chair and excitedly pointed to the exits we should take to escape kidnapping. By that point I had 'come to' and couldn't believe what I was witnessing.

When I arrived back at the table where my family was waiting, it was obvious they had just enjoyed the show of their lifetime. They looked worn out from the laughter. Each one was still chuckling as they filled me in about my antics. Even my mother proclaimed that she hadn't laughed like that in a decade. She claimed she knew that I was gone when I dove to the floor in my new outfit and started to swim, performing my 'pick-a-peach-put-it-in-the-basket' side stroke rather than the front crawl as requested.

All the way home I was entertained by my family as each recalled their favourite part. I chalked it up to one of life's memorable experiences and went to bed.

I was late arriving at breakfast the next day because I was inexplicably compelled to stop at every table in the dining room. I just had to tell them about the fantastic show put on by The Incredible Reveen and urged them to buy a ticket before it was too late.

And you know, now that I think of it, I really don't mind going to the dentist anymore.

The Coach's Wife

Football, football, football. Anyone who knows us is aware that the sport occupies a good portion of our year. Both of our boys have played since they were six and continue to this day. Joe played recreationally until suffering a career-ending injury to his neck; luckily, he has been able to stay active in the game by coaching, which he has done steadily since he began teaching. As the coach's wife, I have missed only a few of those hundreds of games. From early in our marriage I knew that I had to lessen my expectations of Joe during the season, since all of his time, energy and thoughts were poured into the game plan for the following week.

I knew that all of those small sheets of paper with x's and o's were not representative of his affection for me; I quickly learned that putting in a six-pack did not involve refrigerating my beer for the weekend; and deep penetration in the backfield had nothing to do with me.

Joe takes his commitment to coaching very, very seriously. He claims to have been mentored by the best from 'Mac' during his early days at Bishop Ryan in Hamilton. He can recite passages from Vince Lombardi's speeches and has read books, attended clinics and watched whatever he could find in his quest to be a better coach.

There was a period of time when our football schedule for the week began on Tuesdays and continued daily up to and including Sunday. This covered games at both junior and senior levels in two divisions of high school football, nephew David's university game and finally, the Tiger Cats' CFL game. It was exhausting but it was fun for all of us.

Amidst all of this, I had to get out to watch the Notre Dame juniors, the team that Joe was coaching. I did my best to organize my time so that, depending on field location, I would hit the first half of one game, then head over during halftime to catch the second half of the other. This routine was modified only if one game promised a better and more competitive matchup.

In the fall of 2000, it was playoff time and my plan included shuttling between the Notre Dame-Assumption game and Vince's first round match-up.

I started out in Burlington to watch the first half of Joe's game. Since Notre Dame was undefeated they were the favoured team, but it was still a must-win to move on. Watching from the stands, I was not impressed by what I saw. They were giving up the right side and being repeatedly beaten on the sweep. The quarterback was hesitant in his throws and stood unprotected by his line. The opposing team, however, had a look of hunger from the opening whistle. The more big plays they had, the more Notre Dame seemed to crumble; the more Notre Dame crumbled, the shakier they got and the worse they played. Nothing was working for them.

Time was passing and I had to leave. Although Notre Dame was ahead by a touchdown, I just had a feeling about the 'big MO' (momentum, in football talk). As I headed to the car with my eyes focused on the field, it was obvious that Assumption was fired-up to overtake the home team. Their entire sideline of players and coaches paraded behind the white edge of the field; they were jumping, yelling and high-fiving every good play. By contrast, the atmosphere over on the Notre Dame sidelines radiated defeat.

Joe stood at the edge, arms crossed and head lowered, scowling at what was unfolding in front of him. He was not happy. Behind him, his sideline players stood limply following each play, looking fearful of being toppled from their perch. No thrusting of helmets, no encouraging cheers, and no signs of hope. Their team was about to be overtaken as Assumption was clearly on a roll.

In the car, I pulled up curbside in the end zone. I didn't want to leave just yet. I knew what a loss would mean. Yes, the team's quest to play in the championship game at Ivor Wynne Stadium would be finished, and they would be understandably devastated. But more importantly, it would make it very difficult for me to live with Joe after the loss. Even though we have a house policy that gives you twenty-four hours to either wallow in the misery of a defeat or celebrate a victory, I doubted that Joe's disappointment could be that easily handled this time. If we were lucky the memory might dim by January, but it would not be forgotten. Not ever forgotten.

When Assumption tied up the score, my Taurean nature came out. I could not believe what I was seeing out there. What I lack in football knowledge, I believe I more than make up for in reading the body language of a team. (I also know that dark pants make you look and therefore play better, but that's kind of beside the point.). They demonstrated no life, showed no hunger in their play and the entire team's spirit seemed to have been zapped out of them. And there stood Joe, seemingly powerless to do anything about it.

My breathing increased in frequency and power. I sighed. I sighed again. I sighed repeatedly. Something had to be done. Before I could turn the car off, I leapt out and took off for the sidelines. Have I mentioned yet that I wasn't thinking too straight myself? With the determination of a bull, I charged down the white line and went straight for the Notre Dame players who were standing dispiritedly on the sidelines. By the time I was within fifteen feet of them my pointer finger was firmly extended, setting the tone for my unprepared and unanticipated rant. Joe looked back over his left shoulder, nervously catching a glimpse of me. He threw me an angry look that might as well have shouted, "What the hell are you doing here?" I paid no attention.

I started. "Guys, you look like you're the underdogs out there. You stand here like limp fish when you should be supporting your players. They need your energy, they need to be reminded that your team is the best and should be playing that way."

Without taking a breath (and not daring to look at Joe), I continued along like this for a bit, issuing one last order as I wrapped it up. "Now I want to see some life on this sideline and when I leave I want to know that you won this game!" Without looking back, I turned and headed back to my car.

Well, whether because of me or in spite of me, things did turn around and they won the game. I never did leave my spot in the end zone to go to Vincent's game. I couldn't. I was too afraid to budge. After the game, as I saw Joe and his team head my way en route to the change room, I begged our friend Frank to stay with me, for fear of what Joe would say about my unsolicited sideline display. I waited nervously and winced in anticipation.

He saw me, came over to the car and poked his head in the window. Pulling back, I sat in fear. To my surprise, all he said was, "Thanks for doing that. It was exactly what we needed to get us back in the game. The guys have already asked that you give their next pre-game talk."

Oh, thank goodness. I can live another day.

I did give the pre-game talk for the semi-final game. They won.

However, my encouraging words weren't enough for the final game at Ivor Wynne against league favourites, the Nelson Lords. Even the dark pants couldn't help them with that one.

Joe, predictably, can still recall every play.

Giorgio's Journey

I cannot tell you how often humour has gotten me out of a sticky situation, through a difficult time or over a stressful experience. It seems whenever I find myself feeling certain there will be no humour dust in the air today, I become aware of the good humour angel doing her life's work.

My husband Joe is an only child. Shortly after we were married, his mother died suddenly of a heart attack. Within a year, his father Giorgio was diagnosed with cancer. It was particularly stressful for Joe who regularly shuttled between Oakville and Hamilton to care for his father. Three years later Giorgio passed away. It was a difficult time for both of us.

One of the pre-burial responsibilities we accepted was to put together a 'going away' outfit for Giorgio to be buried in. It was an intrusive task to have to sort through his personal belongings just hours after he took his last breath. But it had to be done.

In the closet we found his favourite suit, which he had had custom made for our wedding. From his dresser, we chose a pair of socks and a pair of boxers which I later ironed. Why I did that, I don't know. Perhaps because ironing is often a stress reliever for me. We found his belt, shined his shoes and bought him a new shirt to be worn with his favourite tie. His outfit was complete.

Giorgio was ready to be laid out the next afternoon for

viewing. Having been on the 'visitor' side so many times in the past we knew it meant spending three long days in the ornately decorated funeral home. We were not looking forward to it. The days would be long and tiring before Giorgio was buried. We would need the support of each other, friends and family to cope.

For nearly seven hours Joe and I greeted people on that first day. Throughout the day we accepted people's condolences, shared the events of the past year, hugged, kissed, cried and sighed heavily whenever we needed strength to continue. At one point I told Joe that I needed a break. Off I went to the back of the room where people were able to sit and chat. I approached a group of Joe's relatives who were huddled together in an animated discussion. Heads were shaking and voices were elevated.

I asked what all the hub-bub was about. They looked up and without hesitation continued to shake their heads … but now it was directed towards me. "Whaaat?" I asked, sensing I was being accused of something.

"Carole, you just don't understand!"

Again I pleaded, "Whaaat?"

In unison they shook their heads. Their disapproval was evident. Finally, one explained.

"Carole, the Italians have customs."

"Yes, I think I know that, having been one all my life."

"No Carole, you don't get it. Last year one of our cousins passed away. She was buried without any shoes. After a couple of weeks I had a dream, and in the dream my cousin was very upset. Upset because she couldn't go anywhere. She couldn't go anywhere because she didn't have any shoes. We all found this very disturbing so when our uncle died last month we slipped an extra pair of shoes in his casket. When I dreamt of my cousin again, she was finally at peace and I felt so much better."

"Okay, fine but what does this have to do with me?" I impatiently asked.

"Well Carole, another Italian custom is that the dead must only leave this earth with new undergarments. Without them, they would not be able to go into heaven. And yes, we know you ironed Giorgio's boxers, but Carole, they're old. It's not right!"

"Whaaat? Please! This is a very stressful time for us and that is the most ridiculous thing I've ever heard. You better make sure Joe does not hear any of this." And I turned away from the murmuring huddle, not at all confident that they would let the issue go.

Just then, Joe headed towards us, saw that something had obviously upset me and quickly asked what was going on. I walked away as they proceeded to repeat the story, only this time in Italian. From a distance, I could see Joe running his hands through his hair as he shook his head. I realized that I was right: this problem was not going to go away.

Later that night we headed for home. Both exhausted, it was a quiet ride. All of a sudden, Joe pulled into a shopping mall parking lot. Ordinarily I'm the shopper and tonight was not my idea of the right time to hit the mall. As he parked, Joe looked at me and said, "I don't believe a word of that superstition. But if there's an ounce of truth to it, I couldn't live with myself."

I comforted him with, "Joe, you do whatever it is you feel you have to do."

Joe went into the mall and ten minutes later came running out with a smile on his face. He ran right up to my window, so excited that he didn't bother to go to his side of the car first. He obviously had something to say, so I rolled the window down. He pushed a bag toward me and announced with great pride, "Carole, I coulda bought one pair for two bucks or three pair for five. I got him three pair!" We were both struck by the absurdity of the situation, and as we drove home we strategized how we would carry out the necessary mission.

The next day I approached the casket where Giorgio lay peacefully. When no one was looking, I placed the package of three brand new pairs of boxer shorts in the right pocket of Giorgio's suit. During the next two days, whenever the air got heavy around us and the reality of Giorgio's death hit us, Joe and I would playfully nudge each other and remind ourselves that everything was fine ... because Giorgio was going to heaven with four pairs of underwear.

For the moment, that was all we needed. We'd smile, we'd snicker and we'd feel better. To this day, whenever we recount the story to others we all enjoy the laugh. Sharing it does not lessen the respect we had for Giorgio nor the loss we felt for his death. We both believe that he would have enjoyed it too.

Too Tense to Toilet Train

Our eldest son's (pretty lofty title for an almost two year old) resentment of our second child started to build from the moment he realized that there was something growing in Mommy's belly. Whatever it was got all sorts of his parents' attention, like lots of loving whispers and pats, and all he knew was that it didn't feel so good. Friends tried to warn me about the inevitable jealousy, preparing me for sudden behavioral changes in our firstborn. I chose to ignore the advice. Books I never read had lots to say about it, but even without the benefit of their wisdom, I caught on early that this new baby was more apt to be welcomed with a tackle than with a tender squeeze from his brother.

I worked on improving his perception. We talked, read books, pointed to other little babies, and I repeatedly assured Dante how much we loved him. Something else that I focused on was getting him toilet trained before the next one came along. Everyone told me I would be so grateful to have only one set of diapers to deal with. I theorized it was not so much a matter of toilet training Dante, but more of just how disciplined and scheduled I could become. It really had nothing at all to do with Dante's inner rhythm of movement but more with my ability to force him to go according to my clock. It was a challenge I was up for.

We tried the stickers. We got the pom poms. We looked at

the pictures in his books. The potty was even decorated with this name in big red letters. Just when I thought I had him convinced of not doing 'poo' in his pants, he would rush over to me flashing both a grin and a bare bum to drag me to his latest deposit ... on the carpet in his room. It was tedious, but eventually I was able to proudly announce (to the score keeper in the sky) that Dante was finally trained ... no more mini adult sized diapers, no more soaking stained undies and certainly no more poop 'n scoop off the carpet.

Baby number two finally arrived and wow was he cute! So much hair. Such big brown eyes. And what a smile. Surely a newborn couldn't have that much gas! Since it was summer we had many visitors, and to be honest there was an awful lot of coochie-cooin' going on. Throughout this period we did our best to balance the attention. It didn't help matters that we had a major renovation going on at the same time.

By mid fall it became obvious that Dante was not happy. He played mostly by himself. We were afraid to leave him alone with the baby for fear he'd 'vroom' the truck over Vincie's head or try to wrestle him down (life has always been a contact sport for my boys). By December another major behavioral change developed. Dante's toileting practices shifted dramatically. Was it laziness? Was it forgetfulness? Or was it simply a matter of I'm gonna make them pay?

Every accident saw my frustration rise and my tolerance fall. But I remained resolute. No way was I going to start getting out those multi layered padded undies again. No, I was going to hang tough on this one. Each time he informed me about something stuck in his pants that he didn't like, I tried to invent yet another technique to help deal with this problem. Should I let him wash his own? Hmm, maybe I should at least wait until he's five. Should I let him stay in the dirty pants until he couldn't tolerate it any longer? Too risky, besides I couldn't tolerate the smell. I was clearly at a loss.

Not being one to go to parenting groups, read books spouting the latest trends in childrearing, or God forbid talk to my friends and family about these things (I treasure them as my break from reality), I had to resort to my own creative devices. One day after another I'd hear him cry, "Mommy, I need you!"

I lost it. I loomed over him with the extension out on my index finger. I wagged that finger in his direction until he was dizzy. Before I was able to inform him of his rights, he reached out, grabbed my finger and pleaded, "Please stop blowin' those words in my eyes."

He had me. I knew I was failing the parenting test once again.

A few weeks later, just after Christmas, the situation had not improved. I'm not sure what inspired me, but suddenly I came up with what I thought was a great idea. I looked around the living room at all the new things Dante had received from Santa. I saw how his eyes lit up at the sight and touch of each one. I knew I finally had the winning numbers on my ticket.

I approached Dante and lowered myself to his eye level (to balance the power, let's be fair about this). Adult to adult, I began. "Dante, I know how we can help you to start using the toilet again. See all the new toys that you love so much? Mommy has decided that each time you choose to do poop in your pants, I am going to take one of your toys."

My desperate brain was assuring me this is great! It's only going to take one day to solve this problem. Dante stared back with one curled eyebrow. I was too busy gloating to see his heels digging into the carpet.

Day one I got the Fisher Price airplane.

Day two I got the fire truck.

Day three I got the entire Dinky Toy collection.

Day four, when I took his teddy, I was ready to call Children's Aid on myself. But I stuck with it. (Wonder where Dante gets his stubbornness from?)

Day five I took Blankie and could barely tolerate the pain

inside me.

Next day, Dante looked at me with his big eyes and asked defiantly, "What are you going to take now, Mommy ... my bed?"

I said my prayers, asking for forgiveness. I was at a total loss.

The next week I found myself at the doctor's office with both of the kids. As I waited for their check-ups to end, I decided it was time for professional help. My creative ideas had failed me. I definitely needed some outside assistance. I seized the opportunity to outline the situation to my doctor. He listened and then assured me that Dante really just wanted to please Joe and me. He continued, "Dante knows what is expected. He knows what you want. It's just that it has become stressful for him." As we prepared to leave he suggested, "Why don't you just let it go for awhile?" and concluded with the consoling assurance that Dante would definitely enter grade nine wearing a pair of boxers.

Next day, I dropped the boys at my mom's. I reminded her about the strategies in place, updated her on the current situation and recounted what the doctor had said. When I returned from my errands, my mother welcomed me with a look of triumph on her face. Dante huddled behind her, awaiting my reaction to his accomplishment. My mother announced, "Carole you won't believe it. We were sitting here having some tea and Dante blurted out, 'Quick Nona I gotta go poo!' So we rushed upstairs, got him in the ready position and he did what he had to do. I was so proud of him. We were clapping and kissing. Even the baby was excited. When we flushed, he looked up at me and said, 'You know, Nona. The doctor says it's stress.'"

When I heard this I had my first good laugh in many months. But I also had to deal with an uncomfortable lingering truth ... that I was the reason for the stress. Thinking back about how all this had gone down (no pun intended) I wondered whether my strategies for success might need a little tweaking when it was Vincie's turn. Could Dr. Spock have a little washroom wisdom to offer after all?

Big for My Age

I have always been bigger than everyone else. Since I was a young child everyone around me has seemed delicate, petite and pint sized in comparison. When I was in grade three and earned the report card comment: 'She's a well-rounded student', my ever-so-sensitive brother assured me that this just meant I was fat.

Many incidents contributed to my self-perception of being too big. I once took ballet with my best friend Teresa and my sister Sharon. When it came time for the recital, they danced the roles of graceful flowers and I was a tree ... planted. For any concert or carnival I was ever in, my mom had to custom-sew my costume. By the age of ten, my feet had already reached an embarrassing size ten and a half. When I had to kneel at the communion rail, I purposely moved my shoes in wiper-like fashion to make sure no one could read the size imprinted on the soles. Like they even cared... which illustrates my hyper-inflated sense of self at the time. Once, when a teacher said to me: "Act your age not your shoe size," I was confused. And oh, so frequently I would hear the promise, "Don't worry, honey, you'll lose that baby fat."

I'm still waiting.

So I have endured comments, looks and the poor judgment of others for most of my life. It wasn't just the circumference of my body that drew all of this, but also my height. You see I somehow inherited great length of hands, feet and body, and towered over my friends and classmates. Fortunately for me, I was both athletic and very outgoing, so I had little trouble being picked for teams or making friends. In my little insular world, I really had it made. Every day was fun and everyone I met was quick to laugh with me.

It was when I was removed from this safe, secure world that I became the target of others' unfiltered reactions to my size. Somehow, bad manners and rudeness became acceptable behaviours for people who felt the need to share their comments about my looks ... in particular, my size. Staring back at those pointing fingers, and hearing and feeling the jabs was hurtful. I felt isolated, alienated and very much alone. I wished so much that I could just be smaller, like my sister.

I distinctly remember one particular night. It was 'date night' and my plans for the evening included going to the Roxy theatre in Cooksville with my parents. As my mom and I waited in the lobby, my father approached the ticket wicket and announced: "Two adults, one child, please."

He returned to the line where my mother and I waited and handed the tickets to the ticket collector (who had obviously inherited the job, because she exhibited no skills for her front-line customer service role).

She looked at the tickets, glanced up at us and barked, "Where's the child?"

My dad responded, "She's right here," as he jerked both his head and thumb in my direction. Actually, it was just half a thumb. The other half had been cut off in a baking accident.

The ticket taker took one look at me and bellowed for all to hear, "If she's twelve years old, I'll pop popcorn for the whole place!"

At this point my mother pitched in with, "Well you better start poppin' lady, because she is twelve years old."

The woman then stepped back for a better look and snapped, "Well, she's awfully biiiiiggg isn't she?"

My mother, now full of controlled indignation, curtly retorted, "She's just big for her age."

There I stood, frozen in embarrassment. As I shrunk into my shoes, I made an attempt to slouch as low as I could manage. On my way down, I pictured 'big'. I didn't see the faces of my petite friends. Instead, I'm staring at images of Mac trucks, elephants and buildings. Oh, I so desperately wanted to be small. Before my slipping body completed its slouch, a loud suggestion rose up from behind: "Johnny, you're twelve. Stand up beside her ... my Lord, she is a big girl!"

At that moment, all I wanted was to disappear through the hole in the ozone that wasn't even there yet.

Well, time passed and I matured with it, deciding along the way that since there are parts of me I can change and plenty of others I can't, I should just get on with life. And I did. I accepted that I was not the same size as most others and managed to live my life with confidence. I got that 'good job' with 'good money'; I married that great guy, and happily lived my days. Then, when we were both twenty-nine years old, one of my friends had a baby. At the time I remember thinking whoa, are we old enough for this? I knew that I definitely was not. I was waaay too young for such an adult responsibility!

Joe and I headed off to Joseph Brant Hospital to see the baby. There we stood in front of the nursery pressing our noses into the window. We poked the glass and cooed with delight over Marcia's daughter Carla. At the time, I noticed an older woman beside us holding a similar position. She suddenly looked directly at me and blurted out, "Is this your first grandchild too?"

My eyeballs popped and my mouth hung. I was too startled to respond. All I could do was look back at her. There was no comeback, no friendly response, just a look of bewilderment. Joe realized a sensitive button had just been pressed and that I likely required some assistance. He put his arm around me, looked at the woman and advised her, "Lady, you'll never know the damage you've done. And I have to live with her."

I stayed silent the whole ride home. It wasn't until I got a chance to study myself in the mirror that I noticed a few grey hairs ... okay, maybe more than a few. I immediately went to Joe and, pointing to my head I asked, "When did this happen?"

He gently informed me that it had been happening for a while but perhaps I was too busy to notice or just wasn't paying attention. The grey hairs were still vastly outnumbered by the black ones, though, so I reassured myself that the lady in the nursery was just extremely short sighted.

Well, things only seemed to get worse for me when I got pregnant. Heading to the first prenatal class on my own, I was centered out and asked if I was certain I was in the right class, as the seminar on cholesterol was in the next room. Another day, when I dropped by the Shirley K Maternity store looking for an outfit, I was asked if I was buying something for my daughter.

And I can't tell you how often I was on the receiving end of similar comments once we had children of our own. Each time I would get that lonely 'little big girl' feeling, I wanted to retreat to a safer place. In this vulnerable frame of mind I was unable to respond smartly or offer my typical flippant retort. No, all I would usually do was smile meekly to mask my insecurities, look at my kids and say, "Come on kids, Nona will buy you an ice cream."

I responded this way for years, until one day in the park it all came together for me. There I sat on the bench, watching my three kids play around me. I noticed an older woman sitting beside me. I knew right away she wanted to say something to me. She wore that puzzled expression which indicated she was trying to determine the best way to approach me. After a few stuttered starts she blurted, "Are these your daughter's children?"

I wanted to quip, "No, they're my mother's." But catching myself before I shared my 'humour with an edge' with her, I thought of my mother and somehow gathered the courage to respond with great confidence: "No. Actually, these children are mine. I'm just big for my age!"

At that moment, I felt liberated. I wasn't upset. I wasn't defensive. I did not resort to sarcasm. I had somehow found the courage to shed a new light on the situation. I left the park that day with a smile on my face because I was empowered.

As I arrived home, I immediately announced to Joe with both arms high in the air: "I have made it!" I felt the confidence. I vowed that I would no longer be squashed by others' errors in judgment. I had come to terms with a longstanding source of stress and had even managed to laugh at it.

There have been so many times since that day in the park when I have been on the receiving end of similar deflating comments in reference to my hair colour. Although I still cringe and feel confused by their misperception, I often look back to that first afternoon for strength. With a few deep breaths, I manage to re-inflate my self-esteem and be 'big for my age' one more time.

Uh Oh ... Mommy's Cooking

Whenever Joe was away, the kids and I typically tried to stay busy and often would spend time at my parents ... anything to avoid being home and face the challenge of having to cook. One Sunday, after enjoying an outing with my dad, we returned to my parents' so I could pick up the kids. My mom had already begun to prepare dinner and was strongly encouraging me to stick around. At every chance she'd throw in a dig about me not knowing how to cook anyway, so we might as well stay.

But that day I was tired and anxious to get home. I thought I might be able to fool the kids into going to bed early so I could too. I figured I could at least manage a quick round of Kraft Dinner while scoring big points with the kids. I also saw it as an opportunity to redeem my reputation, since the only other time I had announced that I would be cooking, Vincie, at two-and-a-half, had quickly put me in my place with, "Mommies don't cook ... just daddies."

Clearly, this kind of thinking would not do.

So I turned down the invitation and went about trying to round up the kids. Alena started to cry. How dare I not stay when Nona was cooking her favourite meal ... gnocchi? I was just too tired to stay, and besides I always ended up having to clean my mother's kitchen while she and the kids flipped yet another worn page of the Toys "R" Us catalogue. I just wasn't up for that. So I held firm and managed to succeed with the kids, only to have my mother continue with: "Oh, you! What can you possibly feed them anyway? I'm surprised you feed them at all when Joe's away."

Of course I couldn't let this one pass so I countered with: "Well, I was actually thinking of a little bit of bread with some water."

Refusing to let myself be swayed by Alena's tears, I finally managed to gather the three kids and all of their possessions into the car. On the way home I decided to stop at the bakery for some buns (maybe subconsciously I was thinking ... get a dozen buns, pass them around and hopefully they'll stuff themselves so much I won't have to cook). The buns were so fresh we had to open the bag. As each of us gnawed away, three-year-old Alena suddenly started to cry through her chews.

"Alena, what's the problem now?" I barked into the rearview mirror.

Her mouth filled with bread, head heaving and tears rolling down her cheeks, Alena managed to stutter, "I guess when we get home we get the water?"

Well I did feed the kids Kraft Dinner that night and we did all get to bed early. Mission accomplished, but my reputation for cooking still needed some work.

Put it in the Compost

For years before the word 'recycling' was created circa 1966, my father tried to teach us about its value. We ignored his theories and laughed at his efforts, dismissing their importance. We continued in our long, established and wasteful ways. We carried this behaviour with us when we became homeowners, blindly contributing to the heaps of garbage already overwhelming the local dump.

In the spring of 2001, we learned my dad had cancer and that his health would slowly decline. In the earlier stages, it became obvious that he would not be strong enough to manage his garden. I announced that it was something I could at least attempt to do for him. So I started. In the beginning, it was under his watchful eyes, as he stood in the yard and barked instructions at me. "Save that twine. Dig out those bulbs so I can replant them in the fall. Don't throw that out. Put it in the composter."

As he weakened, he'd position himself by the kitchen window, ready to rap his cane on the pane to get my attention as he watched me work outside. Often the cane would be pointed animatedly in the direction of the composter. Slowly I caught on that nothing was to be wasted.

Even after he was no longer watching, I knew I better damn well do it right because he'd find out wherever he was. I plodded along, learning as I went and tossing all debris into his compost bin. Really, I was just using it as a container for what I didn't want. I clearly had no idea of what it did or how it did it. Right up until his death at home, in his room overlooking the garden, I would continue to ask him, "What am I supposed to do with that composter? You have to tell me what I should do next. I've stuffed it ... now what?"

I never got an answer.

This was not the only burning question that needed answering. I pestered him about the geraniums that he managed to nurse into perennials year after year. What was I supposed to do with those? My family and I actually joked about this state of affairs and my dad's refusal to address them, insisting to each other, "He can't go until he tells us."

We waited. He said nothing. He passed away keeping the info to himself.

Whenever I thought about that composter, I sighed with exasperation. I didn't have a clue what to do with it. Right through the fall cleanup, I continued to stuff that bin. Anyone I asked just shrugged their shoulders because they were as ill informed as me. In November I finally bid goodbye to the garden to allow it (and me) to rest over the winter months.

When I returned in the spring I was afraid to lift that lid. I had recently overheard two women talking in a coffee shop about their composter woes. I leaned towards them, trying to steal any info I could, but all I learned was that it attracted some animals. When I finally mustered enough courage to lift the lid and check on the status of its contents, I was worried about what odour or moving thing might present itself. I noticed as I leaned away from it that although the bin had been overflowing in the fall, it was now only half-full. When I cautiously poked my head in it, I could not believe what I saw. Heaped within the bin was dark, fine soil, rich enough to toss right back into the garden it had come from.

I had to chuckle at my discovery. My dad had had a plan. He never intended to tell me what to do with the compost; he wanted me to figure it out for myself. What a beautiful lesson it was.

That day I made a decision. I emptied all of the soil back into my father's treasured garden, then cleaned the bin and transported it to my own backyard. After that my own obsession started ... coffee grounds, banana peels, wilted lettuce, even lint from the dryer went into that bin. I was hooked. I put a small strainer in my sink to catch the shavings; I watered it; I stirred it up weekly; I let the air get at it to improve circulation. To this day, I continue to be fascinated with the process and marvel at my dad's commitment to the practice of recycling long before it was trendy to do so.

It has been eight years since my father's death but I am certain he is pleased with the progress of recycling. He could have written all of the manuals and led the information seminars. If only we had paid greater attention along the way, it wouldn't have taken us so long to figure it all out.

No Fun Allowed Here

My mother was an active member of the PTA when we lived in Thorold. I remember her heading off to the regularly scheduled meetings and coming home to fill us in on some of the activities they had planned for us. I was proud of her involvement and looked forward to the day when I, too, would get to be one of those 'P's in the famous acronym.

When Dante was in kindergarten he brought home a flyer announcing the first PTA meeting of the year. A special invitation to attend was extended to the new parents of the school, in hopes of attracting fresh bodies and blood. As I read the flyer, I thought back with nostalgia to those earlier days and decided that if the PTA was good enough for my mother, it would be good enough for me. Besides, I really needed a night out. I envisioned it. I'd wear something casual, nothing fancy. And I'd sit at the back of the room, close to the door so I could make a quick exit if I didn't like what was going on.

The night of the meeting I walked over to the school for the seven o'clock start. Entering the foyer, I read the sign: PTA Meeting - Please Follow the Arrows. They led me to the library where, in the eleven o'clock position, sat just three people around a table. As I entered the room, they looked up. Oops, I think I'm in the wrong room. Just as I turned to leave, one of the three called out, "Wait! If you're here for the PTA, please join us. Come and take a seat."

Little did I realize that those three simple words, 'take a seat' carried far greater meaning than just lowering my rear end down onto a chair. I quickly learned that what they really meant was, 'please take a seat on our executive'. Out of politeness and regard for my young son's reputation, I heeded their instruction and joined them at the table, but I squirmed mightily as I tried to convince them I was not interested in being on the executive. I would, I explained, be a willing helper but please, no high powered position for me.

By the end of the meeting, however, I had accepted the responsibility of writing and producing the newsletter. At least it was something I could do on my own, in the privacy of my home office tucked in the basement beside the laundry room.

Months passed and the feedback showed that everyone was enjoying the newsletter, especially the element of humour I injected into each issue. I decided to write anonymously, which allowed lots of freedom for risk taking in my submissions.

After some serious solicitation of more members and numerous months of fundraising, we found ourselves at the last meeting before the annual Fun Fair. The fair was scheduled for the upcoming weekend, when the new playground ribbon-cutting ceremony would take place. The agenda for the evening was full, as were the four tables for attendees. The principal called the meeting to order.

He started with, "I'd like to welcome all of you to our last PTA meeting of the year. We have a lot to cover tonight, but before I begin, I do have a concern to share with Carole." Then, speaking directly to me, he continued, "Carole, you know we have enjoyed you this year. You truly were the freshness we needed to resuscitate our small group. We have especially appreciated your efforts with the newsletter. I think we would all agree it's been a real boost for morale and we all look forward to reading it each month. However, (uh oh) Carole, I must mention that last month when I asked you to include a blurb about our search for a secretary for the PTA, you chose to write it up like a classified ad, citing that 'no shorthand would be necessary and that coffee making skills were not required'. Unfortunately, not everyone got your attempt at humour and we received at least three calls asking about the compensation package offered."

As I listened to his monologue, I told myself to just shut up and take it. Now was not the time to erupt and respond. So I squelched my urge to make a wisecrack. I made a silent note to self to appeal to the seventh grade level next time I had to write something that needed to be clearly understood by the adult readers.

Interpreting my silence as remorse, he moved on to the first item on the agenda. He read us a letter that he had received, voicing concerns about the use of balloons at the Fun Fair. A group of parents was obviously troubled by the fact that these balloons were intended to be loosely tied to a child's arm, wrist or finger. They feared that one could inadvertently be released and float upwards into the sky. They went on to speculate that it could easily find its way into the 'Y' of a tree, entice birds to it and eventually lead to their demise. I pictured a woodpecker hovering about the area and, seeing the bright orange piece of latex sitting in the tree, thinking that lunch had presented itself. Going for it, the latex would burst in the poor woodpecker's face, thereby smothering it to death. I couldn't believe something as bright, fun and lively as a balloon could lead to such a tragedy. And to think that until now I had believed that balloons were intrinsically good things.

Next on the agenda was a brief presentation by the grade seven teacher. She put forward a request that all outdated books be removed from the library shelves, arguing that the notions behind the classic fairy tales were utter nonsense and certainly not what we should be subjecting our children to in the current day and age.

Oh, this one struck a sensitive chord in me. I was a product of reading those wrongful tales. I had been heavily influenced by their outdated messages. I was that little girl who clung to the dream that maybe, perhaps, there was a slight possibility that I could be that princess who figured so prominently in the stories. The one who would not have to concern herself with such trivia as an education or the kind of boring career that was de rigeur in my early days, the very one for whom the only expectation was to pack a small bag of belongings and venture to the outskirts of the forest to wait for that charming, handsome and ever so caring prince to ride by. Who, as he approached me, would catch a glimpse of my exquisite beauty from the corner of his eye and pull excitedly on the reins of his white horse shouting, "Whoa, whoa there buddy!" Then, with the strength of Attila the Hun, he would lean over to hoist me up, maybe calling for some assistance along the way to help elevate me to the coveted seat on the saddle of life behind him. And together we'd ride off into the horizon with him blowing promises back into my face like, "I will serve you and honour you, protect you and love you for all the days of our lives."

I bristled at the audacity of her demands. It was getting more challenging to refrain from reacting to the succession of issues that had been presented. But I held in there, chewing my tongue and weakly making another mental note to examine the content of all those well loved books at home for potential flaws.

One more presentation to go. The grade two teacher stood to plead her case that as parents, we had a responsibility to monitor the violent TV programs that our kids were watching. She specifically referred to my own boys' personal favourites: *Power Rangers* and *Ninja Turtles*. Did I look as guilty as I felt? The only peace I enjoyed after school each day was when they sat together and watched those two shows. It was only after the shows were over that they tried to beat the crap out of each other. My mental notepad was overflowing. I took a deep breath and exhaled to vent my growing frustration.

Finally, just one more agenda item and I was already preparing my congratulatory speech to self for keeping my mouth shut and bull-like Taurean tendencies at bay.

As the principal proceeded to outline the plan for the ribbon cutting ceremony, a parent raised her hand and interjected.

"Please put me on record now. Before we have any ribbon cutting ceremony for the new playground, I strongly suggest that we place a sign at the bottom of the slide that reads NO RUNNING UP THE SLIDE."

That was it. I could no longer contain myself. The bull had been let out of the ring and was ready to charge with vengeance. I jumped up from my seat like I had been ejected. With index finger high in the air, I began to rant, "Why don't we just put up a sign at the front of the school that screams NO FUN ALLOWED HERE!"

Rather than slither back into my seat in embarrassment, I turned on my heel and headed out the door, vowing that my PTA days were over. Although I had disappointed myself with my outburst, I knew it had been necessary for me to say what I did. Judging by the comments in the parking lot the next day I was gratified to learn that I had spoken for many.

I did not keep my vow. I returned the following September with renewed energy for the PTA. But I had marked my territory. They knew how I felt. I was even willing to be on the executive … to champion the fight for fun.

No Testimonial from Me

I exercise most days. Although I prefer doing an activity or playing a sport to hard-core workouts in the gym, I still subject myself to the torture. In fact, I gather a lot of material from the gym.

I do my regular workout in one hour, no shorter no longer. I try to vary the routine and even create some new stuff to keep the boredom at bay. I am constantly on the lookout for any new activity that promises to be the antidote to aging and am prepared to try anything once.

Aerobics were okay. Loved the music, enjoyed the sweating but somehow whenever the class was going left I was heading right and when they were reaching up, I was down. I just couldn't get in sync. Besides, there was always some miserable looking middle-aged woman staring at me from the mirror. I was later horrified to learn that that woman was me.

In an effort to rid my body of post-baby fat I even signed up for a series of sessions in which I was hooked up to electrodes which provided a zapping effect that was supposed to stimulate the burning of fat and enhancement of muscles. I had so much faith in the results that were promised in the TV Guide ad that I would inevitably treat myself with a bag of chips on my way home.

I even endured a stint working with a personal trainer. But when she informed me that I had forty-three percent body fat,

I was so depressed I lost all desire to continue. Was she trying to encourage or discourage me?

I have tried the rhythmical movement class called NIA. Unfortunately it was on my fiftieth birthday and I was wearing a thong for the first and only time. At one point, as I extended my body in expression of my inner spirit, my thong moved. And I froze. I thought for sure it had travelled to another part of my body, never to be found again.

Belly dancing was interesting, especially when I learned that I finally had the right body type for something exotic. I only tried pole dancing in the privacy of my home, but the hockey stick gave me splinters in places I couldn't get at. Circuit training was fun because the leader was easy to look at but when I rolled off the ball, kneeing myself in my nose and breaking my glasses, I never returned.

Yoga. The only appealing thing about yoga is the comfort of the pants. Yoga was waaaay too serious for me; besides, I couldn't do most of those moves and the guy in front of me in those short shorts, shouldn't have.

Then I tried hot yoga. Sauna yoga might be a more apt description. At least with my body heated up I could distort my limbs in ways I never thought possible. When the one and only class I ever attended was over and the endorphins had showered my insides, I felt absolutely elated. When I feel elated, it means I'm happy and when I'm happy I want to share it with the world ... but the kind of exuberant emotional expression that I am partial to was not particularly welcomed by the subdued, inner focused yoga types who had been my classmates. No way, not allowed. My method of showing positive feelings had no place in that studio, nor in that locker room and absolutely not in that lobby. Outward expressions of joy were only acceptable once you hit the parking lot, which was way too late for me.

In my never-ending quest for fitness, I once read about a new technique that involved vibration. Just reading about it got me excited. My earliest memory of a fitness machine involved such a contraption. You remember the old Vic Tanney days? The machine you stood on wearing a belt around your middle which, when plugged in, shook you silly but kept your hands free to eat and drink? There was definitely a lingering result from this strenuous form of exercise: the itching you were left with once it stopped. Nonetheless, when I read about a new studio called Good Vibrations I just had to try it.

And I did. What fun that was. The workout lasts about fifteen minutes and you can do it in your street clothes. Its premise is that you can exercise your whole body by changing your position on the platform while the machine vibrates your body. Doing it with my friend Dian on the machine next to me, the one-liners were flying. Not only were we shaking the fat off, we were laughing our asses off too. We kept our favourite position for last. It required us to sit on the platform, legs spread out with soles of the feet together. With the machine cranked to the maximum level of vibration, we completed the workout joking that all we needed was a drink and a smoke before calling it a night.

You think that one's good? Get this: last year as I marvelled at the newly sculpted bodies of my friends Tina and Lou, I was intrigued by their means of obtaining them. Tina introduced me to the techniques she was practising by inviting me to a free trial one evening. We entered a woman's home in the suburbs and were led downstairs to her makeshift studio. Her sales pitch started as I took off my shoes at the entranceway and didn't finish until I felt the door close behind me three hours later. She started by telling me about her former life and the mess she had been in both physically and financially. In her search to improve her circumstances she read about a new weight reduction technique, and before she knew it she was trained, certified and equipped for customers. She enthused about the success of the technique and advised me that I would need two and a half hours of treatment divided into three separate parts. Wow, and this was all for free?

Once we were in the basement surrounded by the machines

and paraphernalia, she asked me to scan a few info sheets and sign a waiver. By that point, she was citing testimonials of her various clients. Each had lost from three to thirteen pounds after just one session. Heck, one woman dropped a dress size. Surely, a diuretic must have been involved? Imagine going home even two pounds lighter!

Just the thought of getting back into my favourite jeans made me eager to get started. I was excited about the possibilities this session promised. To serve as a reference point and provide a set of numbers from which she would later subtract, she weighed me and recorded the total. I was so keen to embrace this program and do whatever it took to make me shrink a few sizes, going public with the poundage didn't bother me.

Part one involved stripping down to my underwear and having her attach a number of rubber patches all over my body. She then connected me to a series of electrodes using a strand of small wires. As she snapped each one into position, she told me what to expect. I would feel regular tweaks to my skin, which meant that the fat was being zapped, thus stimulating the muscle to develop. Painless, really. Although I had been unsuccessful with this type of procedure in the past, I remained optimistic that this one would work. I breathed through each shot of electricity to my skin, focusing determinedly on the benefits that would be mine at the end.

Next, she introduced me to a bulky looking piece of equipment that was apparently used and endorsed by Madonna. *The Madonna.* We all know how fit she is, so I stepped onto it visualizing my new physique. With a flick of a switch, my entire body shook from tip to toe. I couldn't focus in front of me for the vibration in my eyelids. My teeth rattled, my body fat fluttered and my inner thighs clapped. It was a whale of a workout and I could feel the inches dropping off my frame. I was concerned that I hadn't brought a belt because I was sure my pants would be falling off when I left.

Stepping off the machine, I couldn't wait to see what Part Three offered. Back into the room deep in the basement, she once again asked me to undress. She proceeded to rub a cream all over me and then wrapped my entire body in a plastic like Saran Wrap, the purpose of which was to contain the heat. When she was satisfied that I was sufficiently covered and I resembled a sausage in its casing, she had me lie on a table and proceeded to envelope me in a heated blanket. I stayed that way, melting away the pounds for at least forty-five minutes.

Finally, the two and a half hours had elapsed and I was ready for bed. With a final pitch for her product and procedure, she handed me a package of material and an offer of a ten percent discount. Only thing left to do before I was released for home was the final weigh-in to calculate the success of the evening. I couldn't wait to see how much weight I had lost. Still chattering, she also seemed excited to see the results.

Onto the scale I stepped. I took a deep breath, exhaled the last of any reluctant fat cells still clinging to my body and waited with great anticipation for her announcement.

"Hmmm. Interesting. This has never happened before. But you've actually gained 2.5 pounds."

"Whaaat?"

I laughed out loud and shook my head in disbelief. I got dressed and followed the maze out of the basement, with her clinging to my heels and trying desperately to explain the disastrous results. And as she did, she upped her offer. She wanted me back. I could have three free sessions plus the discount for further sessions. She was determined to see success. I was determined not to be a schmuck again.

The next day I was resignedly back at the gym, surreptitiously competing with the jogger on the treadmill beside me. My quest for fitness continues.

A Job Worth Doing ...

When I married Joe he was a 'fix it' kinda guy. He taught woodworking and also enjoyed it as a hobby. As well, he showed a keen interest in improving our home. That was then.

To get Joe to change a light bulb now takes three weeks of nagging, a whole lot of huffing and puffing, and the kids have to be around to help him retrieve the tools he needs. Actually, it has made me very resourceful. The only task I typically shy away from is electrical work. But that's not to say I haven't changed an outside bulb in my bare feet on wet grass!

Earlier in our marriage, it used to be a fun weekend activity to take on a project together. Like when we built the deck. At the tail end of a three month summer reno, I realized that with Labour Day coming up, Joe would no longer be available to me. With teaching and coaching football, the majority of his time and energy was accounted for. So, I put the push on for the last project of the summer to be the building of the deck.

Plans were drawn up, supplies ordered and tools assembled. We worked a full day with Joe giving the orders and doing the heavy stuff, and me basically providing him with whatever he needed. At the end of the first day I stood exhausted, closely examining our efforts. Albeit tired, my hawk eyes detected a slight spacing problem with the main boards. Hmmm, I don't think I can live with this imperfection. I decided to plead my case with Joe.

Already in bed and barely conscious, he assured me that it would be fine and instructed me to just not look there. I wasn't satisfied. I continued to hound him without success. As a last push of effort, I punctuated my concerns with, "Joe, my father always says that ... if it's a job worth doing, it's a job worth doing well! And besides, I just don't think I could live with that!"

Browbeaten and ticked off, Joe spent the next day lifting and repositioning every board. Through the heavy sighing he uttered, "Stay outta my way ... just stay outta my way!" I slowly tiptoed in reverse to heed his command.

Hours later the finished product had earned my approval.

Two weeks later I took on the very tedious task of wallpapering a small bathroom in the basement. The wallpaper was a striped pattern, which I figured would be easy to work with. I started the job at eight o'clock and at well past midnight I was still trying to make sense of the stripes (I think the guy who drywalled had a crooked eye). I was tired and feeling the stress of the task.

Before heading off to bed, Joe dropped by to check how I was doing. "Honey," he purred, "this corner is out of alignment and my eye immediately goes to the crooked lines. I just don't think I could live with it."

On his way out he threw one last dart, "And as your father always says, a job worth doing ... is a job worth doing well!"

Teacher Interrupted

$\mathcal{O}$ne of my favourite jobs was being a camp counsellor at Camp Tawingo in Huntsville. It reminded me how much I loved kids and especially how much I enjoyed working with them. It seemed to draw the 'teacher' out of me. Whether it involved something as simple as pointing out the difference between the white oak leaf and the red or demonstrating the J-stroke in canoeing (even though I had just learned it myself), I loved being able to introduce them to new things and feeling like it might have a positive impact on them.

At Christmas in 1975, I had just returned from travelling after having graduated from university, and found myself in need of a job. I wanted something that would last until the following summer, when I planned to take off on another adventure. A friend told me about a position in the Phys. Ed. department at Bishop Ryan High School in Hamilton and suggested that I apply for it.

Remembering my fondness for working with kids, I followed up on the suggestion. I found myself feeling both psyched and scared when they hired me for the second semester: psyched because I was going to be teaching girls' Health and Phys. Ed. and scared because it included a coed class in Religion.

It was unnerving to learn that my first lesson in Phys. Ed. required me to teach the somersault. I had only tried to do a somersault once in my life and that was when I was nine years old. On that occasion, when I tried to roll into the rotation my head got swallowed up by my fleshy belly and I thought I was going to suffocate. Needless to say, I was not inclined to try that again and successfully produced an excuse slip of some kind whenever I got wind that somersaults would be involved in a gym class. Luckily, since I was now the teacher I got to ask a volunteer to demonstrate. Isn't that what teaching is about, resourcefulness?

The Health class was the best as we had our own portable classroom and from the beginning, the rules that I decided to set for the class were accepted with enthusiasm by my students. When the course work was covered, it freed us up for stories and camp songs. This proved to be a very successful formula for all of us.

The Religion class was a lot less fun and considerably more challenging. My stomach churned with anxiety before each class as I struggled to recapture my knowledge of the basic tenets of our faith. In time, however, even that experience was enjoyable. It was safe to say I was loving my classes and the students were loving being in them. It proved to be such a case of mutual admiration that we all dreaded the arrival of the end of the semester.

In June, I received a memo stating that I would be evaluated by the superintendent in each of my classes. Even though I was only there on a 'letter of permission' contract, which meant that I did not actually have a teaching degree, they felt it was important to assess my work in case I chose to pursue the vocation later on.

No problem. I discussed the situation with my girls and we were looking forward to the evaluation. For my Health class, I studied the course material, prepared for the lesson as I usually did, came up with a few creative ways to present it and let the rest take care of itself. The class went beautifully and the girls were happy to help out. For Phys. Ed., it was basic basketball skills, which was easy for me and fun to teach. It, too, ran smoothly with everyone 'getting it' and eager to perform for the evaluators.

When classes were over for the day, I met with the principal to review the evaluation. For Phys. Ed., although no suggestions were offered for improvement, I was criticized for wearing pants (a matching velour top and bottoms sewn by my mother I might add). The evaluator felt it would have been more proper to have worn a skort (that's not a typo; there actually is a garment called a skort). Anyway, had I ever considered this option I likely would have summarily rejected it, given the attendant leg-shaving requirements and all.

The only comment contained in his report about my Health class was, "You do not belong in a classroom. You belong on the stage. I suggest you pursue a career outside of teaching."

Ouch. His critique humbled me and his words hurt. He clearly was not impressed with my innovative teaching techniques. I was mortified because I realized that if I ever did choose to be an educator those words would forever remain on record.

Sometimes now as I stand on a stage in front of hundreds of eager faces in the audience, I silently thank him for his suggestion. Although I still believe in my heart that I would have been a damn good teacher, I guess my career ended up going the way it was supposed to go. I now have the luxury to be both informative and entertaining. It's a formula that has worked for my audiences and me for over thirty years. And I get to wear whatever I want.

Viva Italia

Both Joe and I are purebred Italians. Although my mom was born in Canada, my dad had his start in northern Italy. Joe's parents did not venture over until 1949 Joe always said he was stamped in Italy but delivered in Canada. Growing up, I definitely knew about my roots.

Although it was not fashionable to flaunt your heritage in those days, it did help that I spent my first ten years in Thorold, a community with lots of Italians. It was home to a blend of nationalities, and many newcomers seemed to settle there.

In Thorold, it was totally acceptable to arrive at school after having attended yet another weekday Mass and toting a breakfast of fried egg sandwiches soaked in both yolk and oil. There, almost everyone had a nonna, and if they didn't, they wished they did. There, we learned our vowels before the consonants since most of our grandparents ended all their words in a vowel anyway. And there, no one blinked when you had to say your father's name was Peo in front of the whole class.

We regularly visited back and forth with the Ferroni clan, my mom's family in Hamilton, and hiked up to Sudbury at least a couple of times a year to visit the Bertuzzi branch. Family held high rank for us, right after God.

I learned by watching and listening to our aunts and uncles as they shared their lives and exchanged their views with each other. Many a visit would end in a fight, but upon departure the hands would be extended, shaking in a truce. Everybody knew that the issue would never be resolved, but that didn't stop them from hauling it out again the following weekend. They used the intervening week to rethink their side of the argument, develop new strategies and replenish their supply of IPA beer.

When we moved to Mississauga in 1962, we suddenly found ourselves part of a minority group. When I looked up and down the rows of my new grade five class, I noticed that there weren't many of 'us'. One boy for sure, and a few who at least looked like us only with darker complexions. But the ethnic divide became evident later on that first day of class when we were asked for our father's name. After hearing the names Jack, John, David, Michael and Tom repeatedly, I found myself mumbling when I had to say Peo. Every head turned to check out the foreigner. This feeling of alienation passed quickly, though, when my teacher announced that he too was from the Niagara area and was proud to be an Italian. Phew, I was going to be okay.

Like my brother and sister before me, when I entered high school I made the hour-long journey to the only Catholic high school available. It seemed that every European family within twenty miles had also made the decision to send their daughters to St. Joe's and sons to Michael Power. There were numerous pockets of different cultures: Ukrainian, Polish, Lithuanian, Italian and a whole slew of Irish.

Although we naturally gravitated towards our own kind, we were not shy about blending the flavours. In my group of friends there were many non-Italians, and they were quick to spot the differences between *us* and *them*. They marveled at our lunches packed with heaping 'sangwiches' (Sandy's were the best) of salami, capacollo, mortadella and on special days, veal cutlet. They loved meeting Nona and imitating the way she spoke, and laughed at the words of wisdom she shared with us. They couldn't believe how often we were unable to go out because of having to attend a wedding or a funeral. Some of them had never been to either in their entire life.

But the one thing they could not get over was how noisy our homes were. Initially fearing that the shouting was in anger and meant that we were fighting, we had to assure them that that was just the way we communicated. They eventually got used to it and learned that if they were joining us around the dining room table, they had to talk quickly, talk loudly and talk whenever a thought crossed their mind or they would never be heard. Some of them even got good at reaching the unspoken goal of overtaking the other talkers at the table.

My sister and I always vowed that we would never marry Italians. We were proud of our heritage, but weren't keen to continue some of those traditional ways and means that Italians had of relating to each other. Of course our oaths came to nothing. We both ended up with Italian husbands.

Shortly after Joe and I were married, his widowed father suggested we visit Italy with him. We were happy to accept. I was very excited to be 'going home'. I couldn't wait to discover my roots and learn about our family histories, especially since Joe's family and my mother's family came from the same tiny town. At one point during our visit I had to urge Joe to stop probing the people we were visiting for so many details. I was truly afraid that we would find out that we were related.

Upon arriving in Italy, I was set on learning more about the human nature of us Italians. I wanted to discover more about how we live, how we communicate with each other and why we are the way we are. As an enthusiastic people-watcher and reader of body language, I was ready to absorb my findings.

But after arriving it didn't take long to realize just how Canadian I was. It was clear that the 'we' was going to have to be replaced with 'they'.

Physically, although I had *la faccia* of the women in the hometown of Porto San Giorgio, my near six-foot frame towered over them. It was not uncommon for town folk to stop, point and stare up at me as we walked along the streets. One time a woman pushed her children towards me to get a closer look. I didn't know what to do as they hovered around my legs and stared towards the sky where my face was. In northern Italy, where the Bertuzzis are from, I had their size but not their colouring or facial features, making me a true blend of north and south.

Coming from a Canadian town where no one ever saw your underwear, under any circumstances, and if they did, they better be clean, I was astonished in Porto San Giorgio to see the most interesting array of 'mutande' you could hope to find hanging cheekily in full view draped on lines that spanned between windows on each side of the street. I wasn't the only one who found this amusing; the colourful display drew lots of attention from passengers in cars and on scooters below. They were likely hoping to catch a glimpse of some cute lingerie, but more often than not had to be content with a view of more serviceable garments.

Italians have a completely different concept of space than we do. Sitting around the table for dinner, no matter the temperature, it was one continual wrap of skin as each diner stuck to the sweat of the person beside them. And we thought we were noisy. Oh my, it's nothing until you hear it in Italian. Some words dance out, some are spit out, and still others get shot out of a cannon.

Italians are not a nationality interested in rules, whether it involves driving in a car or waiting in a line. Somehow the notion of calm and orderly, one-at-a-time, first-come-first-served, wait-your-turn approach to life must have gotten lost in translation. If a Fiat can pass between the curb and the house without knocking the nonna over, it will; if the speedometer goes as high as a hundred and sixty, then it must be okay to reach it; if the light is just a little bit red and it might be possible to make it through, why not; if there are only three lanes but the cars in them are small, go ahead and fit between them.

Waiting to enter a gym to see a basketball game one evening, I learned that there is no point in wasting time lining up. If you just press your body into the crowd and push with the rest, eventually bodies pop out the other side.

Going for a swim in a public pool in Canada, the first thing we find ourselves doing is reading the list of Do Not's prior to entering. After all, we wouldn't want to break a rule. In contrast, when we visited the pool in Italy, this is what I saw. There was just one lonely (hardly) but lovely lifeguard. Surely he must have been named something exotic like Gianluca. He sat lounging over a chair with a collection of beautiful young women hanging off him. They ate pizza and drank from bottles and cans. Everywhere I looked, bodies were being tossed into the water, people were chasing their friends around the pool and more than one guy in a string bathing suit was making crucial adjustments.

Let me expand on that last practice. During my stay in Italy, I saw more than my share of men with their hands in the vicinity of their crotches. A tug, a quick fondle, an outright hold on a part of their body that we Canadians dare not even glance at. And it doesn't matter where they are when they opt to check on their packages. They could be waiting for a bus or strolling the boardwalk. It's as common as scratching your chin.

My earliest exposure to Italian was from Nona, but that just really covered the bad words. When I was in grade two, my parents arranged for a woman in the neighbourhood to give Italian lessons to my brother, sister and me. I don't think it had the desired impact, though, because the only thing I remember learning was, "Buon giorno, Signora Maestra."

Later on in high school it suddenly became cool to take Italian. Mrs. Speciani's class was a popular one. We learned some expressions that came in handy when referring to the activities that occurred on some of the girls' dates. Phrases like *niente di vestito*, s*olamente baciare,* or *in braccietto* provided an invaluable code for gossiping about how far along the relationship had progressed that particular night.

As dismal as my ability to learn Italian was, I did manage to remember *vieni qua* (come here) because I heard it so often from Nona. For emphatic delivery, she'd throw her hand out and scoop the air and then you'd know she meant it. However, the day I went to the beach in Porto San Giorgio to meet Joe's aunt where she rented umbrellas, I became confused.

There she stood with Joe as I walked towards them. I could see her smiling and hear the words vieni qua but as she uttered them, her hands gestured as if to say *get the hell out of here*. So I stopped in my tracks.

When she barked more emphatically, "Vieni qua!" I took a few steps closer, only to have her shoo me away again.

Joe finally said, "Carole, get over here."

"But Joe, she keeps sending me away!"

He explained the differences in the meaning of the gestures. Paradoxically, pushing your hands away from your body is not a sign of rejection, but rather an invitation in that part of the country. Go figure.

I also had to get used to how often you got touched by Italians' hands or rubbed with their bodies. Words are not spoken without a poke, a stroke or a pinch. Because of this, they only speak when standing close enough to be within a hand's reach or arm's length of you. Although I was initially uncomfortable with this space-invading, close-talking kind of behaviour, I eventually let myself relax and got right into the intensity and intimacy of this way of communicating.

As the trip continued, I paid attention to the Italian lifestyle and their characteristic love of food, good clothes and fast cars. I learned that there was little emphasis on saving money, and that much of their income was spent on enjoying life and looking their best. They lived according to the intangible ideal of *'la bella figura.* This notion refers to how people look and things appear, dictating that it better be good or people will talk. To this day we haven't figured out who those people actually are.

I witnessed first-hand the tight bond of families, often extended to include even the fake wannabe family members, the hangers-on who eventually earned a spot at the crowded table through their persistence. And that young adults, no matter how old, never seemed to leave home until the promise of marriage was at hand (a tradition that Dante reminded us about after we recently told him he would have to pay rent if he wanted to keep living with us. It didn't work).

I was enlightened by the entire travel experience. I learned a lot about Italian culture and history, and discovered that as a Canadian, I could learn a lot from 'them'.

Joe and I have been diligent in incorporating the Italian ways into the upbringing of our children. We have successfully and proudly blended our heritage into our lives and shared it with our friends. No matter their nationality, everyone loves Joe's Italian cooking, both the flavour and the quantity. And interestingly, on many occasions, we have heard one of the kids reassure their friends … "Oh don't worry about all the yelling. They're not really fighting."

"Been There, Done That, Got the T-Shirt"

I have always been the recreation coordinator for our family (I knew that university degree in rec would come in handy), and have done my best to get us to any great event happening within travelling distance. I wanted us to experience it all and have fun while doing it. Of course, in my naivety I somehow thought the kids would both appreciate the effort and remember each experience. One summer though, after enjoying a full slate of activities and travel, I realized that my efforts weren't exactly getting the desired results. I asked the kids what their favourite part of the summer had been ... unanimously they agreed it was watching *Ghostbusters* on TV.

Since basketball was one of our favourite sports, I knew that we would have to be in the stands when the FIFA World Basketball Championship came to Copps Coliseum in Hamilton. I made the arrangements and was able to secure enough tickets for all ten of us to go (my sister's family always joined us on these special outings). We couldn't wait to see the USA Dream Team in action, in particular Michael Jordan, Shaq and Scottie Pippen. The kids all wore their special jerseys, which I had scooped from the bins in the outlet store at a satisfying fifty percent off.

We were all very excited to be there. Our seats were good and we could see all the action from way up in our corner perch. There was also a huge Jumbotron at one end in case we needed a better view or a second look. The kids devoured every aspect of the game and courtside antics. At half time, a crew of highly charged young people ran onto the floor and gestured to the crowd that they would be tossing out some t-shirts. Hmm, I thought cynically, fat chance they could actually throw one this high up into the stands. But we quickly realized they had something to boost their throwing power. Out came a bazooka-type implement that they stuffed with a t-shirt and proceeded to aim towards the crowd. Wow, when they released that thing it propelled the t-shirt into the air with such force they could have shot it across the city.

Seeing there was now a slight possibility that one might reach us, I urged the kids to stand up just in case (you always want to be ready and in position to receive something that's free, whether you need it or want it ... my mom taught us that). So, up we got with hands outstretched and waving frantically to get their attention. They stuffed, aimed and shot. Hey, it's headed our way! In the excitement of the moment, and determined to get a piece of that cloth, I reached out and extended my body to its limit. With fingers in star position, I leaned just a little bit further out from my seat, my shins pressing against the seat in front. The shirt was mine to grasp. As I squeezed one corner of it, I felt a tug from another direction. Clearly, someone held the other corner with equal determination to claim possession. I was not letting go and in the force of the struggle, I lost my footing.

In a split second, my body lurched forward in the direction of the opposing tug. And then I landed...one row down, two seats to the left, right in the lap of a stranger. Completely up-ended, I now had to fight my way back into position. Finally managing to raise my head from the man's crotch, I stared determinedly into his eyes. With disgust he snarled, "If you want it that bad, you can have it." Assuming he meant the t-shirt, I gently snatched it from his grip and called for help from my family behind. It certainly wasn't the kids who came to my aid as they cowered in embarrassment at their mother/aunt's persistence, but they were all over the t-shirt once I had safely returned to my seat.

After this exciting but embarrassing display, I cringed at the thought of what had just happened and quietly retreated back into the safety of my seat. I fervently hoped that no one had gotten a good enough look to identify me and that those around us would soon forget the incident.

The game ended with Team USA beating Spain 115 - 100. We quickly headed to floor level, hoping to catch a glimpse of the big guys. As we huddled around waiting, I saw my friend's son, Teddy. He told me where he had been sitting. It was on the opposite side of the stadium from us.

"Hey, Carole, it was a riot watching you fight over that t-shirt. That guy sure looked ticked when you landed in his lap!"

Surprised by his comment and wondering how he knew, I asked, "You could see it from way over there?"

"No, but when they put it on the Jumbotron everyone was howling."

With sunglasses on, collar up and under a borrowed hat, I grabbed the kids and sheepishly headed to the car.

The Pink Leather Gloves

I love leather. I have a weakness for vibrant colours and I'm a sucker for a bargain. Combine these factors with a good fit and it's a 'must have' for me. So it goes without saying that when I came upon a pair of pink and orange leather gloves in my favourite local bargain store one year, I just had to have them.

I loved my gloves. They coordinated beautifully with my hats and scarves and I got pleasure from looking down at my hands and seeing the bright colours in the middle of a dreary winter. So you can imagine the disappointment I felt when I went to get them one night and they were nowhere to be found.

Although it might not be evident to the casual observer, I am an organized person. I have a routine when I enter the house and there are designated spots for keys, purse, coat, scarf etc. But as I searched everywhere that night, there were no signs of the bright pink and orange. I retraced my steps of the previous day and prayed to both St. Anthony (misplaced items) and St. Jude (lost causes). Didn't find them.

I scoured my life with the intensity of an addict hunting down a fix. I eventually remembered the possibility of placing the gloves in a bag that had then been used to collect garbage. The garbage truck had been by that morning, which meant that my gloves could be gone forever. Oh, how I missed them.

What would I wear to brighten up my winter coat? How could I possibly replace them? I'll never find a pair like them again. Unashamedly, I mourned the loss.

The next day I left for a week to volunteer for Habitat for Humanity in St. Bernard Parish, an area outside of New Orleans still suffering from the effects of Hurricane Katrina. Within minutes of our arrival at the airport, I saw the impact of that storm and the scars left by the broken levees. As we drove closer to my destination, it was obvious that some areas had been harder hit than others. I could not divert my eyes from the devastation surrounding me, each sight conjuring up feelings for the families affected by this disaster. I tried to imagine what they had gone through and what they continued to experience amid the destruction of their homes, neighbour-hood and entire city.

On my second day there, I was placed on a team with six other volunteers and assigned the task of gutting a home. It was a brick house that had not been touched since both Katrina and the ravishing flood waters had left their imprint a year and a half before. I was not prepared for what followed. In the place where a welcome mat had once been was the outline of a skeleton, which we later learned to be of a deer that had landed on the roof and then fell to die.

After pushing in the front door (the key, which had been left in the slot, is now in my office at home as a reminder of my experience), we were met with a stench so intense it left us gagging and reaching for our masks and gear that was designed to cover every inch of our skin. The only way to describe what we saw upon entering is to ask you to imagine this: When you arrive home tonight and open the door to your home, you discover that somehow while you were out, your home had been picked up, given a good shake on all sides, and then placed back down with walls and roof intact. Every other morsel of your world, your home, your belongings and your treasures are now but a heap of debris mixed in with eight inches of mud, fallen plaster, fermented mold and the residue of polluted floodwaters.

Over the course of the day as we cleared the home down to the studs, we slowly pieced together the fragments of the lives of the two women who had lived there. We found medication for diabetes; gourmet recipe collections for the ardent chef; rolls and rolls of wool; religious artifacts, shoes, shoes and more shoes, bank receipts, diplomas, bibles, books, CD's and linens bagged and ready to pass on to another generation.

The young people with us that day attacked the job with great intensity and little emotion. The three of us middle-aged moms on the team were less willing to ignore the devastation within our sight and each of us reacted to it in different ways. One was emotionally affected by the collection of Depression glass lying scattered and broken all around; one needed time in the kitchen as she sorted through a collection of recipes and I stood motionless by the linen closet thinking about the family linens that had once been safely stored away. As we grappled with our feelings, we got on with the necessary task, treating all of these once treasured possessions as garbage to be carted out to the curb. What started as a neat pile eventually became one massive heap of debris, as we tossed item after item out the front door.

Out went boxes of memorabilia, prized collections, favourite pieces of clothing and everything else once deemed valuable. We did manage to salvage a small number of items that we thought the homeowners might want and placed them to one side of the heap for safekeeping. When we returned from lunch those, too, were gone, now in the hands of a scavenger hoping to make a few dollars from the salvageable debris.

I am still not over the images and the feelings I experienced during those few days. I will not forget what I learned first hand from talking with the survivors or from what I saw at every turn. Although I am left feeling grateful for what I have and fortunate for the life I enjoy, I am ashamed of my own attachment to the things in my life. I moan and complain about a twelve dollar pair of gloves while the families I met have lost everything. Rather than mourn their losses they concede that both faith and family are what they now treasure. They do not mention their photos, trophies or favourite pair of gloves.

I can't promise that I won't try to replace those gloves, but I do know that l now look at the things in my life differently and will be forever mindful of how fortunate I am to have a plethora of the real treasures in life.

P.S. Just last Sunday, I was at a family reunion. My cousin Marylyn came up to me and announced, "Oh nuts Carole, I meant to bring your gloves."

Unsure of what she meant, I asked "What gloves?"

"The ones you left behind at the game that night in Waterloo about three years ago. They're colourful."

"Colourful like patterned?"

"No, I think they're pink and orange."

"AHHHHHHHH."

They arrived in the mail today and surprisingly looked both worn and soiled. In the note from Marylynn, she explained that when her daughter saw them in the house, she assumed they were work gloves so proceeded to wear them for both barn work and gardening.

Perfect. I think I too might just wear them for dirty work now ... and I'll do it with pleasure.

Under the 'B' for Bingo Bus

Developing a taste for Bingo from my mother, I learned to enjoy it for what it was ... a game. A mindless game requiring no prior experience or skill level beyond recognition of five letters and seventy-five numbers. All you have to do is block out all distractions and take direction from the caller, making sure to keep tabs on potential wins. Sometimes four corners count; sometimes it's the travelling 'T'; but most often it's a simple line in any direction.

When I first travelled to the east coast of Canada by thumb in the 1970's, one of our overnight stops was in Moncton, New Brunswick. After a cheap dinner and with no plans for the evening, Teresa and I decided it might be fun to drop by the local legion. We had noticed a sign on the way into town: BINGO Tonight - Jackpot Must Go! So we headed over and walked in, drawing more than a few long stares as we looked for a spot to sit.

Clearly, we had walked in on their fun. The caller stopped mid-call, all heads shot up and hundreds of eyes followed us as we claimed our seats. You could hear the mumbling and the whispers. Feeling more than a little conspicuous, we lowered our heads and whispered instructions to each other about how to proceed. Trying not to draw any further attention to ourselves, we quickly got set up and joined in the game.

I guess it became apparent that we were from 'away' because the other players stopped looking at us and resumed discussion amongst themselves, probably about us. A short time later, one of the ticket sellers stopped at our table to have a few words with us. He must have been the designated snoop because he started right in with the questions.

"So, where you two young ladies from? Ever visited this here part before? How long you figure you'll be around?"

We chatted a bit and politely provided him with all the information that he needed to share with and pacify the others. Eventually he was called off to sell some cards and we quietly resumed our game.

Just prior to the intermission, the caller made an announcement.

"I'd like to take a moment here now to introduce two fine young ladies from Ontario. So let's give them a warm eastern welcome and help them feel at home."

And they did. Surprised and touched by the sentiment, we waved at the appreciative crowd, feeling more than a little self-conscious about all the attention.

By the time we left the hall that night, we discovered what east coast hospitality is all about. We had an invitation to dinner; a friendly couple offered us their cottage on Shediac Bay; one friendly fisherman offered to take us out on his boat and more than a few suggested we drop by to meet their sons. That experience endeared both Canadian easterners and the game of Bingo to me forever.

After that, whenever I visited a new town while working or on vacation, I checked to see if there might be a game going on while I was there. I discovered that it was a great way to get a feel for the community and to meet the people who lived there.

A few years ago, I travelled to Newfoundland for a vacation with Joe and our friend Linda. It was a chance to visit Brian and Jane who had recently bought a home in Ferryland. Having visited the island a number of times in the past, I had a simple list of what I wanted to do while I was there. My plan was to spend my time living like a local in Ferryland, just doing the things they enjoyed doing. That way I knew I would get a chance to feel like part of the community and meet the wonderful people who call it home.

I did my best to do it all: daily visits to the hardware store to chat with Charlie and the other salesclerks; tea with Maxine as she shared Ferryland lore with us; hanging out with Rhonda at her coffee shop, the Ferryland Cafe, and enjoying her singing; playing baseball with the girls and hitting as many kitchen parties as we were invited to.

The days were full and I was meeting a lot of beautiful and talented people, but there was still one activity I yearned to do. I desperately wanted to go to a Bingo game. When I announced this to Maxine, she immediately said, "Well, you don't have to go far. We play it on the TV set and call in our Bingos."

When I expressed doubt that it could be all that much fun, she assured me that it was a social highlight of the week for many, and they didn't even have to leave their homes if they didn't want to. Some folks even had a standing date to gather at someone's home, where they would have a few drinks and play together in front of the TV.

She described the format. One caller, one helper to post the numbers, an image of bouncing balls and a phantom telephone to take the Bingo calls. Kind of bizarre, but I admired their island ingenuity and appreciated the fact that all proceeds went to the church. I listened politely but said I would still rather get a taste of the real thing.

Then she remembered. "Yes, yes, okay. There is a Bingo, but it's thirty-five miles away, over in Witless Bay."

"Really, why so far? It must be difficult for people to get there."

"Well it's run by the church down there. But there is a Bingo bus that picks people up. It travels along the shore between Fermuse and Tors Cove. It makes stops along the highway and drops them at Bingo."

"Okay, now we're talking. This sounds like fun. Where do I go?"

She told me exactly where to stand (in front of Kavanagh's Snack Bar), the time the bus would be by (around five o'clock) and how to stop it (just extend a casual wave as it approaches). Jane and Maxine decided to drive down while Linda and I opted for the bus ride. We planned to meet them there.

We were both pretty excited about the ride, and executed the appropriate wave when we saw the bus coming. It stopped without even pulling over. On we got and suddenly all the chatter ceased. The women who had been leaning on the seats in front of them to talk to their friends retreated into their own space. Those sitting alone simply grabbed their handbags, clutched them close to their bodies, and looked out the window as if not wanting to be recognized.

Ooops, I think we might be interfering with their fun. Quietly we decided that we would not make a scene but just sit back and wait to arrive at our destination. Occasionally someone would turn her head as if to check on us and report back with her findings. The driver repeatedly glanced up into the rearview mirror above him to monitor our behaviour. With difficulty, we remained restrained and gave them nothing to be concerned about. Upon arrival at the church, we respectfully waited for everyone to get off the bus before descending. By then we were anxious to meet Jane and Maxine in the church hall so that we could at least talk out loud.

Once we had purchased our cards, snacks and dabbers, we set out to find our spots. It wasn't until we got organized and were ready for the big game that suddenly everyone wanted to know us (they already seemed to know Maxine who, with husband Charlie, are local icons).

Three tables down, the ladies leaned forward to catch our eyes and when they did, they smiled and waved at us like we were old friends. Other folks bypassed the treat cart to head our way and offer a welcoming remark. Some got up from their spots and headed directly to our table to chat. Suddenly we were celebrities. Everyone had a story to tell and a laugh to share. Okay, now we were having fun.

We didn't win anything that night but all the way home, as we drove down the centre of the highway (just in case there were moose), we relived parts of the evening and listened with interest to Maxine as she recounted background histories about the people we had met.

I smile every time I think of that Bingo night and the many characters that were part of it. Each of them had their own quirky uniqueness and contributed a charmingly different take on what it is to be Canadian.

Maybe that's what inspired Linda and me to check out our own local Bingo hall and go there for an outing with our friends. We had all been there before as volunteers, back in the days when, as young parents, we did fundraising for our kids' teams. (I have fond memories of stripping my clothes off on the porch before entering the house after my shift because I reeked of smoke).

That first excursion with our friends evolved into a birthday tradition. It started with my fifty-fifth and has continued every few months since. We never win but since everyone around us seems to, we're pretty sure we bring them good luck. Could it be the tiara worn by the birthday girl, or perhaps the fresh smell of homemade popcorn or birthday cake that we bring with us? We try our best not to carry on too much for fear of attracting deadly looks or being unceremoniously shushed (Bingo is, after all, serious business). Mostly, however, we meet up with folks who are keen to help us figure out which cards to play and how to decipher what the caller is saying. Interestingly, it doesn't seem to matter which night of the week we choose to go; we see the same players in the same spots whenever we show up.

We never get tired of giggling at Maryanne's comments or the corny one-liners that Dian, Linda or KSB can't resist making after particular calls (like 'two can dine on 0-69 or 'it's a vitamin' whenever B-12 is called). And Carol Ann still doesn't get why it's funny when she exclaims, "Heavens, I only need twelve numbers for a win."

The truth is, we could care less if we ever win, knowing we'd have to split it six ways anyway. No, our fun starts well before the first number's called and has little to do with ever achieving a full card. We now have our own version of the Bingo Bus and have discovered that the party starts the moment it pulls up.

So Much for No Contact

All my life I have been involved in sports. But contact sports have never been part of the regime. Sure, it got physical in some of the games but mostly by accident and in hopes of not drawing a foul or interference call.

A few years ago, my niece Natalie enticed me into joining her recreational flag football team. They needed a quarterback. She assured me there was no contact, that no running would be expected and that all they really needed me to do was throw.

Throw a football I could do. My brother Larry taught me. I could throw a perfect spiral from the age of ten. Heck, I could even block, as he used me as his practice dummy while trying to earn a position on his high school team. I had the chance to execute my prowess in powder puff games in high school and university, and my skills served me well for meeting guys on the beach.

Natalie was quick to introduce me to her teammates at the first practice. Judging by their initial reaction, I think that when Natalie boasted about getting her aunt to join as the new quarterback they did not envision a fifty-year-old white haired woman with arthritic knees, wearing a brace, mouth guard and vintage bandana. I quickly settled their concerns by throwing them a series of balls landing perfectly in their outstretched hands.

We bonded. I was welcomed onto their team. My membership had bonuses. My sister, kids and nephews now came to cheer. My husband and brother-in-law Richard hung around enough analyzing our coachless efforts that they soon happily filled the vacant coaching spots.

We had plays. Some worked beautifully, others bombed. We even won a few games. While other teams loaded with more testosterone than estrogen bumped chests in celebration of a magnificent play, we happily hooted, hollered and hugged when a mere pass was caught, even if a first down was never achieved. We were having fun and we liked each other. Ah, a recreational participant's dream.

Natalie wasn't completely honest about the no-running-required-clause.

Being the quarterback meant that after the sequence of 'down - set - hut' was shouted, the centre would fling the ball backwards through her legs hoping to send it somewhere within catching distance of me. Once I secured the ball, I had to scan the field for the designated receiver, step back and release, all before the rusher chased me down. If I didn't handle the ball like a hot potato, getting rid of it as soon as it landed in my grip, I was forced to run for my life. However, because of my speed, or lack of it, I never got too far.

In one game Richard, who has both played and coached at every level, was ejected from not just the game or the sidelines, but from the entire park for remaining true to his firm conviction that 'you gotta make that call ref', but failing to communicate it in a way that the recipient found helpful.

We loved him for his passion. I didn't appreciate Joe screaming orders to me from the sidelines, though. After all, these women held me in high esteem and he was making me look bad as he shouted out things like, "Get the lead out" and "C'mon, Sooze, THROW it; don't PUSH it!"

In most games we lacked a sufficient number of participants to adequately field players both sides of the ball (offence and defence). So, one night after a failed series of plays, I was required to fill in the position of centre. It meant that I had to bend over in the tripod position to hut the ball back to Catherine, our kicker. I waited for the directives. At the sound of 'hut', I flung it back to her. Once the ball left my fingers I moved as if in slow motion to reposition myself upright and proceed down the field after it. At least that was my intent. I no sooner released the ball and began to elevate my body than I was met head-on by a huge mass. The rusher facing me had darted towards me with such force and aggression that in my halfway back up stance, she made contact with my face, propelling me backwards onto my back.

As I lay staring at the sky, I was hesitant to touch my face for fear it had been rearranged. I moved my tongue to check the status of my teeth. I blinked to be certain my eyes still worked. And who knew where the glasses had landed. A crowd gathered as I stared up at the gawking faces of concerned teammates. My sister was immediately at my side, simultaneously screaming at the bully who had levelled me while providing comfort to her 'little' sister. I slowly got myself into a seated position, nodding my head to indicate that I thought I might live. My head throbbed, my face hurt and my neck was already stiffening up.

As I wobbled into an upright stance, I asked if we at least got good field position from the kick. Right then I heard the ref call out, "Ten yard penalty on the offense."

Judging by the outcry from my teammates I knew that this meant us. He continued, " … for obstructing the rusher."

"Whaaaat??"

I was livid. He called ME for getting in the way of the person rushing after the kicker; the one who ran me over; the one who showed no remorse for the potentially career-ending injury to my fifty year old body; the one with bigger biceps than boobs?

I was ticked. My retort to the call was, "But you don't understand, ref. I wasn't blocking her. I was merely trying to stand up."

He showed no compassion. I sat out the rest of the game. When it was over, we all hugged and vowed we'd get them next time.

Of course the other team went on to win the championship later that season. Over beer after our final game we enthusiastically toasted our bond with each other, with our coaches Joe and Richard, and to all of the fun we had trying to master the game. Forgotten were the bad calls, the near fights and potential career ending injuries.

I have since retired from the field, but I know that any Monday night I could venture over to M.M. Robinson High School and see the same team chest-bumpin' out there on the field while my old friends whoop it up and high five with girlish glee.

An Act of Contrition

Raised as Catholic, I was educated in parochial schools from kindergarten through to grade thirteen. Both nuns and priests influenced me during that time, and much of my religious training stemmed from the teachings in The Baltimore Catechism. Together with my classmates, we learned each prayer and procedure by rote. This practice often prevented me from reciting prayers on my own, as I missed and needed the supportive voices of the others to lead me. So, I usually just talked to God in my own way.

Over the years, life happened and my practice of faith waned. I developed some opinions that challenged the teachings of the church, had some experiences that affected my thoughts and beliefs and gradually found myself straying from my religious roots.

As time passed I gradually ventured back into the fold with our kids in tow. I had settled the disagreements in my head and found a way to adhere to my personal philosophies without having to butt heads with the church. I may not have been the best practising Catholic, but I trusted that the beliefs and values I lived by were honourable.

Turning fifty in 2002, I chose to commemorate the milestone birthday as I had the others, by celebrating for the same number of days as my new age. When I declared my plan, others assumed it meant a long string of partying. Wrong. My intent was to make each day special in some way, no matter how simple. It wasn't about gifts, cake or champagne and didn't even have to involve other people. My intention was to cover all aspects of my life: physical, social, athletic etc. It was a fabulous plan, and I looked forward to making every single one of those fifty days unique and meaningful.

Nearing the end of the fifty days, I realized I had neglected to account for my religious side. Hmmm, what should I do beyond the regular ritual of going to Mass? I looked into potential retreats but the timing wasn't right. I considered and quickly discounted other possibilities before coming up with the great idea of going to confession. For those who are unfamiliar with this, it involves entering a private cubicle and facing a priest, who sits unrecognizable behind a screen. Using a standard format, the aim of this sacrament of the church is to allow you to divulge any sins you may have committed, in hopes of having them forgiven by the priest. In granting God's forgiveness, it is standard practice for the priest to assign a penance, which often consists of a series of prayers. The penance is like a giant eraser. It gives you a shot at a clear conscience, and the opportunity to avoid sinning again.

According to my calculations, I had not been to confession since 1979, just before we were married. That was a long period of time. A lot of stuff had happened. Thinking this project through, I decided that I did not want to execute my plan locally. A confessional on another planet would have been ideal, but I decided that London, Ontario might do just as well. I contacted my friend Marcia and asked for her help. She did her research. A week later she escorted me to her church, assuring me that nobody would know me there.

Together, we waited outside the confessional for the person before me to finish. Whispering, we decided that whatever he had done, it must have been bad because he was in there a very long time.

We giggled, remembering our own first confessions at the age of seven when, not knowing what sins might be the most appropriate ones to confess, we made stuff up. Unfortunately, in my case, I made the mistake of using my 'outdoor voice' while in the confessional so all my friends could hear.

The longer we waited the more nervous I got. I was struggling to recall the words I was supposed to say. Marcia tried to help but in my nervousness, I wasn't grasping it. Finally, it was my turn. She wished me luck and into the cubicle I went. Unlike the dark, curtained confessionals of my past, this one seemed to have more light. The priest was still screened by the mesh partition but it felt more airy. I started with, "Hi Father. My name is Carole and I haven't been to confession in about twenty-five years." Why I dispensed with formalities and opted for the coffee shop approach, I have no idea.

Looking at the left side of his face through the mesh, with his head supported by his hand, I heard him snicker. "Wow. Well, welcome back, Carole. What brings you here today?"

Phew, he was accepting and he was friendly. Maybe it was my intro that broke the ice, but what followed was a casual conversation about what had happened along the way and why I had wandered off course. He listened quietly as I ranted about the actions of other clergy I had encountered. He did not judge me, nor did he step in on their behalf. It was easy to talk to him and the experience was less painful than I had anticipated. When things were wrapping up, he said to me, "Carole, can you give me an Act of Contrition?"

Remembering that this referred to the prayer you recited to ask for forgiveness, I went to the box in the back of the brain to retrieve it, but found it empty. Its words had been deleted and more than likely replaced with the lyrics to *American Pie*. Where were my classmates when I needed them most? When I told him that there was no way I could do that without the help of my friends, he kindly responded, "Well then Carole, we can say it together."

At that moment, I noticed a business card lying beside the spot where I was kneeling. The words Act of Contrition came into focus for me from the floor. I leaned over to pick it up.

Could this be divine intervention? Sure enough, it had words on it that looked like a prayer. I gingerly extended my hand around the partition and presented the card to the priest.

"Father, will this do?"

He laughed, looked at the card and assured me that it would certainly do. He then asked me to read it to him. With my hand safely back on my own side, I proceeded to read the prayer. It seemed to be a whole lot shorter than I remembered, so when I was finished I said, "But Father, isn't this like reading the Coles Notes?"

Chuckling, he explained, "Actually, it is. This new shortened version has been created to help people just like you."

The confession was sealed with the assignment of the penance. To my surprise, this was not in the form of a string of prayers that could be recited without actually paying attention to the words, but rather a suggestion of something meaningful I could do. I enthusiastically advised him that what he was asking of me was something that I already did every day. That's all he needed to hear. He offered his blessing and thanked me. I left the confessional box in high spirits, my fiftieth day of celebration complete. My slate was clean.

When I returned to Marcia in the pew, she leaned over and growled, "You made that last guy look like an altar boy. You were in there a long time. What exactly did you confess to ... a serial killing?"

When I showed her the business card that had miraculously appeared at my feet, she looked at it in disbelief.

She had a lot of questions. "What is this? Who left it there? What happened to all the other words?"

"It's the twenty-fifth annivesary welcome-back edition. Written just for me."

No Money, No Mappa, No Makin' It Backa

When I headed to Belize in the winter of 2005 to work in a mission, I wanted to take as many opportunities as possible to see the area in and around Benque. So in between my volunteer stints in the church gardens, at the school and in the small town, I made it known to the permanent staffers that I would love to tag along with them whenever they left the town. They were more than willing to oblige. It became a safe way for me to get into parts of the community I otherwise wouldn't see.

During my second week there, I got an invitation to join a small group that was going on an overnight trip to Flores, in Guatemala. I was quick to pack my favourite net bag.

When school was let out for the day, we got a taxi to the border, trudged through the rain to Melchor, the town on the Guatemalan side, and then boarded a bus for a long ride over narrow and bumpy roads to our destination.

Actually, it wasn't really a bus, but an extended mini van with extra benches installed so it could pack in twenty people instead of ten. Because of the rain the windows remained shut, which meant that the conditions inside the pseudo bus were hot, crowded and odiferous. As an added feature, it was dark outside, so sightseeing was impossible. We settled in for the two-and-a-half hour ride.

Arriving at our destination, we quickly checked into a curbside hotel and hit the streets for a festival. We enjoyed the night exploring the town and meeting some fellow travelers. It had definitely been worth the ride.

After a very tough time trying to get some sleep that night, I got up the next morning feeling guilty about missing a day of teaching back in Benque (the guilt came easily ... I am, after all, Catholic) so I quickly decided to return in time for my afternoon class. When I informed the others about my change of plan, they expressed some concern about me travelling alone. I assured them that I'd be fine and asked them how to get to the bus station in nearby Saint Elena.

I confidently hailed a taxi and in my very limited Spanish, told the driver where I was headed. After a short ride, I stood overcome by the noise, vehicles and smells of a busy intersection. Nothing was familiar. Since we had arrived in darkness and rain the night before, I hadn't taken in many details about my surroundings. Seeing the area packed with many buses resembling the one I had arrived in, I was overwhelmed with confusion. To make matters worse, various men were calling out to me, "Quick, quick, come here, this bus!"

As I was being jostled into one of the vehicles by a particularly insistent driver, I pointed to where I imagined the border to be and, with a touch of panic in my voice asked, "Benque? Melchor?" I was hoping that he would recognize the name of this small town in Belize or the Guatemalan border town and reassure me that he was headed that way.

"Si, Si!" he enthused, and in an instant the money was gone from my hands and I found myself inside the bus with a crowd of morning travelers.

Before leaving Belize, I had purposely toned down my travel look in hopes that it would draw attention away from my near six-foot frame and shock of bright white hair, and help me blend in. The long skirt with socks and sandals is not what I would normally wear, and in retrospect might not have been a very good camouflage outfit, but there I was, committed.

Checking out my fellow passengers, I noticed three young children whose eyes did not leave my face. Pressed on either side of me, two weathered looking men enjoyed an animated conversation without seeming to notice that my face was between them. As I bobbed my head to the rumble of the bus, I craned to see if I could recognize anything familiar from our journey the night before. Having no luck, I eventually decided to check with the man beside me, again using the tactic that had previously been so effective for me.

"Melchor?" I asked, vigorously jabbing my finger in front of me.

"Si, si," he nodded with disinterest.

Trusting that we had communicated effectively I was somewhat mollified and turned my attention to my surroundings. The bus made numerous jerky stops and starts along the route, which provided me with an ever-changing mix of fascinating travelers, workers and families to study.

Two and a half hours later, we arrived at what appeared to be the final stop, which I figured out only because everyone was making an effort to get off the bus. As I looked around, I knew that I was definitely not where I was supposed to be. Nothing about this place resembled the border town we had been in the night before. There, fifty yards from our stopping point was a river and along the edge sat shoddy raft-like vessels. People lined up to board them in order to travel across the river.

Being the last one off the bus, I'm sure I looked as dazed and confused as I felt. All eyes were on me and many of them were laughing. Men huddled together, smiling and nodding their heads. They had figured out that I was not where I expected to be and were openly enjoying my predicament.

I approached the driver to ask him where we were, but he dismissed me with a "No comprende," and walked away. I could feel the panic build inside me. I had no map, no command of their language and very little money. Scanning the crowd of faces around me, I settled on a woman with four children wrapped around her legs. There was something about the way she looked at me that suggested compassion. I went to her, wrote MELCHOR on a piece of paper, and showed her my passport to indicate it was a border town. Nodding in understanding, she took the paper from me, wrote SAYAXCHE and motioned me back in the direction of the parked bus.

I gave the paper to the driver. He looked at it, acknowledged the destination and barked, "San Elena," the name of the town where I had come from that morning. He told me how much it would cost to get to where I assumed was Melchor, the border town. I paid him and got back on the bus. All eyes followed me. Not sensing any friendly sentiments among the gawkers, I ignored them and began calculating how much money I had left. Combining my U.S., Belizean and quetzal dollars, my funds were now down to what equaled about fifteen dollars.

I sighed and stewed about the possibility of missing my class as the new bus trip began and the bumps continued. At one point, a trio of weathered cowboys got on. I must have been quite a sight because their eyes and attention never left me. The more nervous I became, the more Hail Marys I recited. I tallied what my belongings might be worth to them: one hammock in my bag, a sweater, a silver bracelet, small studded earrings and a pair of Nikes. Surely they'd settle on the goods before harming me.

After three hours passed (which went without incident, I am relieved to report), the bus pulled into a busy parking lot. We were greeted by more minivans, much yelling and the tooting of horns. To my surprise, we were not at the border, but back in San Elena. Six hours of travelling and I hadn't moved an inch.

Scared, tired, hungry and desperate to pee, I immediately tried to negotiate the trip back to Melchor.

"Si, si." The driver assured me his bus could take me there for twenty-five dollars. I only had fifteen.

I pleaded with him. He walked away, shooing me like a fly. I followed him, trying to make my case but he conveniently chose not to understand. He finally stopped, studied me from head to toe and with a final glance at my white hair (no doubt figuring that I was older than I actually was), he took pity on me and agreed to take my last fifteen dollars. He motioned to where I should wait. Declaring my need to go to the washroom first, he nodded his permission.

I ran to the washroom area and into the rustic cubicle. Ah, relief. Figuring there'd be no paper, I had smartly packed my own and used it. As I emerged to wash my hands, a woman stood in front of me, blocking the door with her hand out.

"For what?" I gestured.

"The use of the facility!" she motioned back.

I argued that I had used my own paper but the hand remained open as she blocked the doorway. I handed her a dollar, knowing I was now going to be short for the bus driver.

Back to my spot to wait for the bus, I was nervous about paying him. Diverting his attention, I folded my money and quickly handed it to him. Without checking the amount, he slipped it into his pocket. Confirming my suspicions that he believed me to be a needy older woman, he helped me into the front seat beside him. But not before placing a beautiful young woman between us.

It had now been seven hours since I had left the hotel and chances were the group I had travelled with was already en route back to Benque. I tried to settle my breathing and relax, knowing that at least I was now headed in the right direction.

With the bus jammed with eighteen travelers, I was happy to have the front seat and a clear view of the jungle we rode through, even though I had no one to talk to. Feeling more optimistic as we meandered along the one lane road, I began to relax and enjoy the view. Not wanting to draw any more attention to myself than I already had, I decided to leave my camera in my bag and just take pictures in my head of the sights I saw along the route: scantily clad families who were busy dragging bamboo leaves, stoking fires and washing clothes by the river.

Unexpectedly, the bus came to a halt. Looking up I saw a long string of vehicles with their doors open. Excited people were tumbling out of the various cars, trucks and minivans. Lots of Spanish was flying about. It was obvious we weren't going anywhere because a twenty-four wheeler had slid off the muddied roadway coming from the other direction, blocking the roadway and preventing any vehicles from passing. Heads were shaking, arms were thrown dramatically in the air and everyone seemed to have a lot to say about our predicament. It would be a long wait.

Venturing back to the first vehicle with English speaking travelers, I stopped to chat about the situation. The driver expressed his doubt that we would be able to move for hours, if then. There was even some talk that we could be stranded in the jungle for the night.

After two hours we were finally able to continue. It was now six o'clock and it would soon be dark. I knew that once we arrived at the border, I still had a ten-minute walk and a taxi ride to reach Benque.

Nervously, I whispered more prayers. Saint Jude (patron saint of hopeless cases) I need you now. Just get me back there, please!

Suddenly something happened that lifted my anxiety and actually brought a huge smile to my face. Yet again, the bus had stopped in the middle of the road, where we witnessed a scene that I wished I could have captured on film. There before us was a piglet who appeared to be in a stupor as he wandered aimlessly across the road, his head wedged inside a large can of pork and beans. We all looked at each other. Finally, the language barriers seemed to crumble as the entire group of passengers erupted into the most comforting round of laughter. I knew then that everything was going to be okay.

At 8:15 I got out of the bus. By 8:30 I was across the border and sitting in a taxi. Without explaining to the driver that I had no money, I asked him to take me to the rectory. I could see faces pressed up against the upstairs window when he pulled up. I asked the driver to wait and went to borrow some money to pay him.

My friends greeted me with relief. They had been nervously looking out for me ever since the other travelers had arrived hours earlier. Once I was safely at the dining room table munching contentedly on what seemed like a feast to my ravenous eyes, I recounted the adventures of my day.

When I finished my story, they sat there quietly shaking their heads in disbelief until one of the priests said, "Carole, you must be very thankful that you arrived here safely. It is all too common to hear tragic stories about unwitting travelers who meet up with the wrong people. Don't you remember the recent headlines about the two tourists who were attacked with a machete for a few dollars?"

Horrified, I thanked God that my story had had a different ending. It now joins a long list of other such personal tales scheduled to appear under the heading "What Was I Thinking?"

Friendship

$\mathcal{I}$ could never have imagined that life could get better after we moved to Mississauga from Thorold. After all, Thorold was my life and that's where I left both a piece of my heart and the only friends I ever knew.

But life in Mississauga, then Erindale, brought new tastes and flavours into our world. First, at my new school surnames ending in vowels were rare. I was accustomed to being surrounded by Italians, and at this school everyone was so Canadian (or as Nona referred to them … *tutti anglaise*). The church, rectory and convent were nowhere close to our school so we played freely, not worrying about the reverend onlookers scrutinizing our behaviour. And my new friends introduced a freshness with their big city ways. Although living well into the suburbs, with nearby Toronto's influence, Erindale was considerably more urban than the St. Catharines I was familiar with.

It didn't take long to make friends. It helped that I was a good athlete, so I was a first pick on their teams. And I was endearing enough that they knew they could have fun with me. So this is how I bonded with my new friends. We were tight, right through to the end of grade school, claiming both the plaza and the park as ours to roam and hang out at.

I considered myself blessed to have such great friends, so I wasn't keen to move on to high school and start fresh yet again. Fortunately I was accompanied by Kathy (her name change came later), whom I admired for her liberated spirit. Knowing she too had to don the heavy black serge uniform and oxfords provided comfort to me. I knew if Kathy could pull it off, I could too. For ready companionship we buddied up with two girls from other nearby schools, namely Paula and Paula. These two had been friends since grade three and like us, were facing the new high school experience with both excitement and trepidation.

Together we would all ride the Greyhound bus to our all girls school ten miles away. It gave us lots of time to create a scene with our antics. We'd people watch and make up stories about each of the riders, all the time breaking up in howls of laughter from the back seats. When we finally arrived at our stop, typically creating one final clamour by a frenzied search through all of our belongings for our ticket stubs, the rest of the commuters surely sighed a breath of relief at the prospect of finishing their trip in peace.

The rowdy behaviour led us past the statues, through the front doors and into the halls of St. Joseph Catholic High School. We were the travellers, the ones who came in from the country. In those days, no one knew where Mississauga was and figured we were all hicks. Until grade eleven I had them believing I lived on farm with a horse named Arthur. We figured we would forever be a group. We had no need to expand. We had each other.

But the very first day of school blew up that notion entirely. Huddled in the gymnasium waiting for our grade nine room assignment, little did we know our world was about to explode yet again. From 9 A to 9 E, the names were called to fill each class. And as we waited to hear our names, we did what females everywhere do easily, readily and often ... we immediately made a connection with each other.

That first day of school marked the beginning of a long list of longstanding relationships. From the safety, security and comfort of our once small group of thrown together friends from the 'country', we opened our arms to a multitude of others.

We all fell in love that day ... with each other. There was Marcia, quietly standing alone not knowing anyone; Babbi who, with her sister Carol just a year ahead of her was more outgoing; Sandy, who being related to most of the Italian population of Toronto, introduced us to everyone she knew; Carrie, an athlete keen to try out for any team with me; Angie, who even in the ugly uniform oozed cool with her other friends from the city. Of course there were lots of others with whom we shared our memorable five year stint at St. Joe's. The ones we hung out with from the teams, the ones from our particular classes and the ones we cavorted with in the 'caf'. It resulted in a long strand of intertwined arms connecting us all as St. Joe's girls.

What was planted that day in September 1966 has blossomed into a magnificently arranged garden of perennial beauties. Each has bloomed at different times throughout the past four plus decades we have been together. Each offers her own unique presence to the mix. All continue to lead fulfilling independent lives, yet forever connected. Some see each other regularly while others wait for the email or call rallying their attendance at yet another opportunity to reunite.

We have worked together, lived together and travelled together. We have brought husbands, significant others and a slew of children into the fold. We continue to enjoy annual outings and although we have all branched out to embrace new friends from various segments of our lives, we remain deeply loyal and committed.

They compose the safety net on which we can each fall at any time, knowing that regardless of what we are going through, who we have become or aspire to be, they will be there to catch and coddle us as needed. Although many of the names have changed from the likes of Babbi to Barbara, Kathy to Kathleen, or Carrie to Carolyn and that most (not all) tend to look different than their grade nine photo, each time we're together we only see the young-spirited and fun-loving girls we were when we all first fell in love.

I Really Enjoyed the Salad

I have always wanted to see Nashville. To satisfy this urge, I was prepared to slap a tourist sign on my forehead and travel there by bus. But as it turned out, I didn't have to. In 2000, I had the opportunity to speak at a conference at the Opryland Hotel. I accepted the booking before they even got a chance to share the details of the event. I was very excited.

My sister Sharon and I have a tradition of taking our mom away on an annual trip, so we decided that they would accompany me to Nashville. The plans were all in place. It would be easy to use the speaking engagement (and the accommodation it provided) as an opportunity to enjoy an extended weekend together.

When we arrived at the airport in Nashville, I was surprised to see a man in uniform holding a sign that read BERTUZZI LUCIANI. Oh my goodness, that's me. This had never happened before. I ran over to him and introduced myself. Very politely he welcomed me, assured me he would take care of the luggage and escorted us to a midnight blue stretch limo that was waiting for us. Wow, this was a first for me.

My mother, impressed by the extravagance of the welcome, expressed her appreciation. Since she paid little attention to my career, she assumed that it was always like this for me. As we left the airport, I considered the pros and cons of telling her the truth. Deciding that it would do little to elevate my status with her, I elected to do nothing.

Arriving at the Opryland Hotel, we were greeted as special guests and informed that our registration had already been taken care of. A bellman escorted us directly to our room, a beautiful suite featuring a king sized bed. Counting three bodies, I resigned myself to the fact that we'd be sleeping like spoons. Not a problem.

As we looked around the room, marveling at its opulence, I noticed the red light flashing on the phone. I picked it up and heard a message that had been left for me. "Welcome Carole. By now, you have been able to see your room; we certainly hope you will be comfortable here. We are soooo excited about meeting you. There is a buzz about you being here and we just feel so fortunate that you agreed to do the closing keynote. Please drop by the conference room when you are settled. We can't wait for tomorrow!"

Wow, what a welcome. Comparing it to some of the feeble greetings I had received over the years, I had to admit that it was a tad over the top. But I liked it.

I decided to drop by to meet my hosts before I headed out for dinner with my family. As soon as I entered the office and saw how excited they were to meet me, I started getting nervous. My thoughts swirled with insecurity. I was undeserving of their welcome. Surely, they had received the wrong 'bio'. I was not the superstar they anticipated. I almost felt fraudulent. But, no, they seemed sincere in their interest and expressed their delight at finally having the opportunity to meet me.

I was told that the conference was going very well and that everyone was looking forward to my closing presentation. They were sure it would provide the perfect wrap up to a very successful event. By the time I left, I was questioning whether I was ready for this presentation. I had a feeling of dread, which was foreign to me. Usually I am filled with anticipation and excitement before a talk. What had I gotten myself into?

I was quiet the rest of the night. I rethought my content. I tried visualizing success but the image was blurred. I second-guessed my choice of outfit. I had a restless sleep with numerous flips of the pillow. By morning, I knew I was doomed unless I could refocus on my task. I finally convinced myself to just go for it and if they didn't like me that was okay because they'd never remember my name anyway.

My sister did my makeup. My mom ironed my outfit...and slowly I reclaimed my confidence.

My keynote presentation was scheduled for 11:00 a.m. and would be followed by a lunch. By 11:05, I had them. In the words of that infamous Oscar acceptance speech, they liked me, they really really liked me! It was a huge success. The standing ovation was unnecessary, but appreciated.

The conference chairperson offered a sincere and heartfelt thank you and as we shook hands asked if I'd join their table for lunch. Dizzy from the post-talk high, I said I would. Everyone around the table was quick to extend their hand and introduce themselves. They hailed from all over the USA and were eager to learn more about me. I was on my best behaviour, exchanging pleasantries and answering their questions about me and about Canada.

The salad was delicious. Lots of variety and lots of crunch. I ate as we talked. After the first course, my brain told me that I was approaching the energy depletion stage, so I decided that it would be best to excuse myself before I crashed. I thanked my hosts for their hospitality and reached out to shake hands with each one as I said goodbye. Such lovely people. The chairperson escorted me to the door. He once again expressed his appreciation of my efforts and mentioned that I had exceeded the committee's expectations. He was thrilled with the finale to the three day conference and gave me credit for ending it on a high note. I thanked him, smiled and headed back to my room.

I was elated. I had pulled it off and done what I was supposed to do! I had aced it and felt good about it. Adding to my elation were the accolades I had received and suddenly my ego was so inflated I had to enter the elevator sideways. Thoughts of success were dancing through my mind. Surely Oprah will be calling any moment.

I unlocked the door to the room, anxious to get out of my 'speaking clothes' and unwind. Tossing my bag onto the floor, I approached the mirror by the washroom to take off my earrings. I reached back to unfasten the first one and gave myself an approving smile. Uh oh, what was that on my teeth? Leaning closer I got the full, horrific view. A piece of spinach, nicely nestled into my gum, had draped itself over the top of my front tooth. A speck of peppercorn was wedged between the two teeth next to it.

Ohhh! Nooo! I looked like I had just come out from the back woods.

My head immediately started to throb. How long had it been there? Who saw it? What must they be saying about me now? I screamed. I cried. My elation evaporated just as quickly as it had appeared.

Then, in spite of myself, I started to laugh, imagining the conversation around the lunch table after I had left the room.

"You should have told her. You met her first."

"No way. Buffalo's closer to Canada than Texas; it was YOUR duty."

"Oh my goodness, that was painful. Someone should have said something."

Knowing they must be getting a sympathetic kick out of my misery, I might as well enjoy it too. The laugh was cathartic.

By the time I shared this story with my mom and sister I had already embraced the comedy of my woe. I eased their horror by recalling with pleasure, a phrase from the movie *Punchline*: "We are merely God's animated cartoons."

But geez, surely one of them could have told me.

Same Window, Different View

My dad lived a life that was both rich in relationships and full with activity.

His days were packed. Somehow he always found the time to do all of the things in life he wanted to do as well as those he had to do. And although he did enjoy his regular rants and occasional gripe fests, he generally aspired to face any life challenge with hope.

By August, 2001, it was apparent that my dad's health was failing. As he got weaker, his mobility within the home decreased. He spent most days in a wheelchair in the living room forced to communicate with a steady stream of caregivers, all wanting to dote on him and make him comfortable. He mourned the loss of the lifestyle he enjoyed for most of his adult life. Now that his future was dimming, he lacked any enthusiasm to continue.

One day as I was watering the front gardens, I went into the house to get something. As I passed the living room, my dad yelled out in my direction "Carole get in here."

As an adult I had learned that my best approach with my dad was to humour him. Most often it worked to soften his edge and temper any foulness in his mood. This day was no different. I heeded to his command and entered the room. There beside him sat yet another stranger with a specialty in healthcare.

I extended my hand. "Hi, I'm Carole. I'm his third favourite child."

My father was not amused and ignored my feeble attempt for some levity.

He snapped, "Look out that window and tell me what you see."

I did as he asked and focused on the view through the large living room window. I quickly replied, "Ah, I see a beautiful garden that I have been maintaining in your absence. And look, you were wrong. I have succeeded in growing impatiens for Mom under the pine where you said the soil was too acidic. Oh, and there's a dog that looks ready to do his job on your lawn. But wait, he's reading your homemade sign with the image of the squatting dog with the 'x' through it. He seems to know that no pooping is allowed there, so he's leaving with his tail wagging and his head shaking."

My father was not laughing. He wasn't even smiling. Nope, there was not a hint of pleasure on his face. He curled up his mouth, shook his head and sighed in frustration. He then let loose. "J**** C**** Almighty, you don't see the G*# damn bird crap on the window?"

I strained for a better look and responded. "As a matter of fact, I don't."

I turned and headed out to the garage to fetch the ladder, which I needed to reach the window. As I did, I started to cry. I realized right then that my father no longer had the ability or the desire to look out the window with optimism and recognize the beauty that was there. And as I climbed the ladder to search, scan and scour the window free of any evidence of bird crap within my father's view, I convinced myself that it was not the time to remind him about all that he had taught us nor to share my own motivational tips with him. No, it was best to say nothing but to accept it as a reminder to continue to wake up each day and enjoy life ... for those who can't.

Bowling for Dollars

*M*y mother is quick to recognize how fortunate she is to have the grandchildren she has been blessed with. The three girls and five boys adore her and display numerous gestures of love and affection in appreciation of how good she has been to them over the years. After all, how many grandmothers have the insight to buy better toys for Christmas than Santa himself; send cards with cash for holidays including Hallowe'en, Valentine's Day and Easter; and have a knack for always finding the rare, hard to locate item on the wish list? She seizes any opportunity to be with them, often inviting them to join her for dinner, whether at her own home or her favourite restaurant. At eighty-nine, my mother has done all of the above with regularity and great pleasure.

One of my mother's favourite traditions is to host an annual bowling outing with her grandsons. They all start out at the Mandarin for a Chinese buffet lunch because she knows she can always get her money's worth with them there. Besides, she enjoys the attention she gets from the wait staff as they comment on her handsome assortment of escorts. After they load up at the buffet, they all walk over to Classic Bowl, which is conveniently located in the same mall.

Once set up with shoes and designated lane, my mom proudly sits there monitoring the automated scoring system in front of her and relishes watching her boys bowl off against each other. Sure, they are competitive, but it is actually my mother who pits them against each other. She is fully responsible for the jostling, teasing and intimidation that goes on amongst them. It's her fault. Why? Because she gives out prizes.

That's right. Days before the scheduled event, you can find my mother sitting at her kitchen table organizing her prize envelopes, each one a mere two inch by three inch beige envelope. She carefully organizes her cash, puts the appropriate amount in each envelope and indicates the standing on the outside. They are then filed away in a safe place until the day of the tourney.

For many years, it was just the four boys because Michael was out of the country. The year he rejoined them, they laughed him off, underestimating the popularity of bowling in China. To their surprise, he beat them all and collected the coveted first place envelope.

We always get a kick out of the stories the boys tell about the outing after they get home. They invariably go over every detail of each game, from the frequency of gutter balls to the strings of strikes. Each embellishes his own performance, with the overall winner claiming bragging rights for the year. Of course, all of this is done in good sportsmanship and with appreciation for the prize envelopes that are awarded.

Until one time when Vince came home harbouring a complaint. Exaggerating his disappointment with his faring that day, he announced, "Mom. You gotta talk to Grandma. She needs some tips on motivation. Look at the envelope I got from her today."

He showed us his winnings. He had come in fourth out of four.

In his envelope was a loonie. And on it was written LOSER. It wasn't that he had only won a dollar, nor was it that he knew that his cousins had received as much as ten bucks. It was more about the way his last place finish was labelled.

We jokingly called my mom that night to complain to the

'judge' about how she had squashed our youngest son's ego by labelling him with such a moniker. She was quick to defend her actions. "Well, he's just going to have to practise if he wants to do better than that. He was awful. I could have beaten him."

The boys love recounting their tales of Buffet and Bowling with Grandma, so much so that this past spring when she was in very poor health they immediately cited concern that they may have had the last of their fun with her.

Fortunately, her condition has greatly improved since then, and they're already making plans to reunite for yet another friendly competition.

But they collectively want to put an end to her secretly giving tips to Vince on how to improve his game, which apparently happens when the rest of them are away from the table for another round at the buffet.

It has been rumoured that they have all been practising (supposedly Wii counts) ... all in an effort to avoid the disgrace of that dreaded last place envelope.

Lights, Camera ... Action?

In my role as Director of Community Relations for the Mississauga Hospital there were many duties I was asked to perform. This made the job interesting because it was so varied. During the hospital's fundraising campaigns, I was frequently invited to attend local functions to accept donations.

Service clubs, businesses, associations ... the routine was generally the same. I would arrive promptly, wearing what I considered my Sunday best, meet the necessary people, grin and wait. Sometimes it would be quick as they would get the 'passing of the cheque' out of their way before hitting the business portion of their meeting. Other times I would sit through an entire ceremony, anxiously awaiting my turn to stand. Often I would then have to pose with the donors, each of us gripping a portion of the cheque, smiling until the local newspaper captured the moment. In some instances a simple 'thank you' was sufficient; other situations allowed me a bit more time and range to my speech. Actually, other than meaning a lot of evening work, it became painless, even enjoyable after a while. I could usually count on a decent buffet and I always met interesting people.

Arriving at this comfortable attitude did not come without some hard lessons learned along the way, however. Case in point: early in my career I was invited to Dixie Arena to accept a cheque from the community hockey association. Just going back to the old arena was exciting for me. Many a Friday night during my teens had been spent skating laps around the ice with my friends as we teasingly tried to get the boys' attention. The familiar smell of hot chocolate mixed with popcorn brought those memories to life.

That night, one of the league officials met me at the entrance. It happened that he knew my father, so that gave us something to chat about as we made our way through the cool wooden paneled corridor towards the locker room. I started to feel a little out of place in my patent leather pumps and wished I were more comfortably dressed to blend into this environment. Along the way, the fellow was proud to point out the various team pennants and photographs displayed on the wall. I was vaguely aware of the legendary history of the Dixie Beehive hockey team. They were always distinguishable by their team jackets and seemed to travel in threes throughout the community.

As we approached the locker room, I got a little nervous. I really had no idea what to expect. I began to hear loud, deep voices and roars of laughter. For sure, I was entering territory oozing with testosterone. Entering the room, I found myself surrounded by an army of team jackets on bodies of all sizes and ages. Team uniforms, more pennants and trophies lined the walls. The portable lights set up by the local cable TV crew standing nearby brightened everything. Whoa! No one had told me it was going to be televised.

Most of the league officials greeted me with gripping handshakes. The energy level and spirits were high. I looked around, feeling like I had shown up at the wrong party. As I scanned the room, I couldn't help but wonder what exactly was going on. The camera guys were in the ready position. Various men were jockeying for place as I stood nervously awaiting direction. I assumed that all of this choreography was for some special award ceremony or team picture.

Finally, the president approached me and announced they were about to begin. Believing that my importance on this roster was secondary, I positioned myself well back in the room (and besides, I didn't want to block anyone's view of the ceremony). Quick signals were given, cameras rolled, and the president of the league approached the microphone. As he swelled with pride, he spoke in length about the history of the league, the teams' successes, the talented young men who had gone through their system, and the legions of volunteers who had given thousands of hours of personal time. He spoke with affection about the building itself, referring to historical data and paying particular attention to the league's important and longstanding role in the community.

Wow! What a speech. I was impressed. I was ready to lace up my skates and buy one of their jackets. Where do I sign up? As I was lost in thought during this oratorical masterpiece, I heard the words, "So, I am very pleased to call upon Carole Bertuzzi Luciani to accept our generous donation to the Mississauga Hospital. Carole, please come forward."

Oh no, I had no idea his speech was the lead-up to giving me the cheque. What about all these other people standing proudly in the throng? Weren't they going to be introduced? Weren't there awards of recognition to be presented first?

At this point, my mouth was as dry as the slivered wood at my feet. My belly started to dance as I dragged my patent leathers to the front. Beaming with pride, he extended his open right hand towards mine while the other participants shuffled into a big hug around the enlarged cheque and me. Responding, I shook his hand and accepted the other end of the cheque.

With a stiff, nervous smile, I offered a very simple, "Thank you very much!"

That was it. I said no more! His eyes continued to beam in my direction as if waiting for me to say something else. My lips were pressed shut. I grinned sheepishly, knowing nothing more was going to come out of my mouth. I stood frozen in silence.

The camera crew held their position as everyone else in

the room remained quiet, politely anticipating more from me. Five, ten, fifteen seconds passed. It felt like an hour. Finally, the cameraman popped his head from behind his lens and announced: "I guess that's it, boys."

Throughout the room, I heard a collective sigh of relief, like air being released from a tire. I then said my personal thank-you's and snuck out of the room.

All the way home that night, I thought about the awkwardness of the situation. Had I adequately represented the hospital? Would they have been satisfied with my behaviour? Surely, they wouldn't have expected me to say more. Well, maybe I should have said a few more words.

All night as I tried unsuccessfully to sleep, the scene played repeatedly in my mind. The next day, I handed the cheque over to the head of the hospital foundation with little explanation. And I prayed no one I knew would be watching Cable TV.

Two days later Joe and I were watching one of the many football games of the day on T.V. In one particular game, there was a special presentation at half time. The presenter spoke with eloquence about the importance of such a donation. After the presentation of the cheque, the recipient took the microphone and for the next few minutes expounded about the generosity of the donor and his organization's appreciation of the gift. He outlined precisely how the money would be used, shared a personal anecdote and concluded with a sincere expression of gratitude.

Joe and I watched in silence. When the speaker finished, I asked with trepidation, "Joe, when someone gives a donation like that, is it necessary for the recipient to say much more than a simple 'thank-you?" A part of me already knew what the answer was and didn't want to hear it.

"Oh yeah. That's the opportunity you have to tell them how much you appreciate their efforts and a chance for you to really connect with them. Any donor wants to know that their donation is important for improving a program or facility or whatever the money is going towards. Why do you ask?"

I let out one big regretful sigh. "Oh, no reason. Just wondering."

I won't ever forget that blunder. To this day whenever I walk by a Dixie Beehive team jacket in the mall, I find myself whispering, "Thank-you very very much for your most generous donation. The Mississauga Hospital really appreciates ..."

The Funsets at Sauble Beach

When we were children, there was little opportunity for family travel. If we went anywhere, it was a road trip to visit our cousins in Sudbury. My father's way of making it different than the last was by changing the route we drove. This was never to our benefit or enjoyment, as he typically made detours to take in more sightings of concrete structures along the way (which was the nature of his work in our friends' family business). Inevitably by the time we reached the shores of Richard Lake we were bored, tired and still scrunched from the four of us being crammed into the back seat of the sedan. The fourth was always our cousin Marilyn who was invited to join us on the Sudbury treks.

Occasionally during those years, we were invited to visit my aunt and uncle at their rented cottage at Sauble Beach. It didn't matter how many were staying at the cottage because we would spend the entire day until sunset on the beach. During the long winters, we dreamed about our visits to see the welcoming arch erected at the main drag.

The love affair with Sauble continued in my teens when we would head off to camp at the provincial park near the falls. Different kind of fun, but it still all took place on the beach.

It was a welcomed surprise after Joe and I married when he informed me that if we ever wanted to rent a cottage, his godfather owned one. It was located right on the beach at Sauble. I jumped (slowly though, as I was pregnant with our first) at the chance to return. Again, we enjoyed full days lounging, walking and enjoying any conceivable friendly competition of games on the beautiful shores of Lake Huron. We have continued this tradition annually since 1985.

The drill is the same. Joe and I rent the cottage. We then invite anyone who is interested to join us. But the real fun doesn't start until Uncle Richie gets there. Somehow, we know the party can finally begin when he shows up with loaded coolers in hand and a cigar behind his ear. Our record for bodies sleeping in the small three bedroom cottage is fifteen, all sprawled in every direction on foam, inflatable mattress, couch or bare floor. The sounds of snores, sighs and other bodily symphonies typically fill the rooms. Who needs a good sleep when you have all day to recoup on the beach?

Over the years we have solved numerous problems of the world sitting there staring at the water; we have given a multitude of newly aquired girlfriends and boyfriends the shakedown (we figure, if they can pass the Sauble test, they're a keeper); we have settled way too many disputes over children crying foul over 'no fair' playing; and we have repeatedly feasted on Joe and Richard's beach meals while enjoying Anne Marie's desserts. It's always a celebration there with no fret, fuss or fancy.

The ultimate celebration occurred in 2004, the year of our twenty-five freakin' year anniversary. Although we knew who would be there to join in the fun, we were unprepared for the fun itself. The planning had been done in advance but the prep began late afternoon when without an announcement everyone ran for their posts. We were informed the proceedings would begin in fifteen minutes. They whisked us both away to get dressed ... me in a pair of satin pyjama bottoms and veil and Joe in his undershirt, shorts and bow tie. Suddenly it all unfolded. A procession appeared of all the young guys in their jammers and cowboy hats, girls in boas and bathing suits. We were led to the beach with our nephew, Christopher, hoisting his knapsack of piped music. There on the beach was an assembly of our weekend guests on lawn chairs neatly arranged in a semi circle. They positioned us before them where we were surrounded by our wedding party of children. Then with everyone standing, the 'officiator' arrived. Wearing a safari hat, swimsuit and tie, Uncle Richie was on hand to assist us as we renewed our vows. His official book was the Sauble Beach and Surrounding Area Telephone Book. He began with the reading of a few passages for us to ponder. Passage one from page 235 ... "Marten, Martin, Martinello, Martini. Passage two from page 331 ... "Peters, Petersen, Peterson, Petric. He then asked us to place our joined hands on the tattered yellow pages of the book to pledge our continual love and affection (more like patience, stamina and endurance) for each other. We concluded with a raucous display of appreciation from our guests, then I turned and flashed my secretly placed 'hillbilly teeth' at the crowd as we trooped up to continue the feast.

We enjoyed lobster that night, eating just fast enough to beat the mosquitos who were hovering for any drip of butter that might escape. Before we got to the desserts, someone appeared. Thinking it was a stranger dropping by to see what all the fun was about, we caught a closer glimpse of the intruder. Sure enough, behind the hat, oversized glasses and black and white accordion stood Richie who proceeded to enthusiastically play a polka for all of us to dance to. As his own kids cringed in embarrassment, the rest of us grabbed a partner and danced around the deck. We had drawn a crowd. Everyone wanted in on the fun.

We can't wait to see what develops this summer at the beach. We have so much to celebrate with three sixtieth birthdays and our thirtieth anniversary. Who will show up? What news will be delivered? Any newcomers to shake down? And what will the weather be like? The truth is that none of it really matters. Because we know that regardless of how many people we have crammed into the cottage, whether it's hot or cold or pouring down rain, we welcome the clutter and the chaos that surrounds us. It tells us we're together in a place we love.

And like every other day we have enjoyed there, we do not leave our spots on the beach until the infamous sun sets at Sauble. As we watch the sun drop off for another day, we always sing the same song ... "Nighty night sun. Thanks for coming out today. Hope to see you to-morrrrrrrrow."

We then pack up our stuff and retreat back to the cottage knowing that every 'next day' at Sauble will inevitably be even better than the last.

Junk Week Junkie

My eclectic taste in home and garden decor is partly a result of being a bit of a scavenger. The practice of foraging for decorative and functional goodies started in earnest when I was faced with the task of furnishing my first apartment on a very limited budget. I enjoyed the mix of unique and nostalgic pieces, which created an environment of comfort that suited me perfectly.

Living in a crowded bungalow with our family of five, it was essential to honour the rule that what-comes-in-goes-out (excluding kids of course). Unfortunately we (okay, I) didn't always adhere to this regulation and at one point, with the house spilling over with collected treasures, Joe announced that our saturation point had been reached and that enough was enough. Pleading my case, I was quick to remind him that one woman's trash was another's treasure. Knowing full well that I was referring to his first failed marriage, he advised me not to change the subject and declared a moratorium on junk collecting. He doesn't always appreciate my attempts to lighten things up.

Therefore, I kept it as a secret from him when our town started publicizing an annual Bulk Collection, which quickly (and more accurately) became known by everyone as Junk Week. This was an event that was indeed worthy of putting on the calendar and highlighting. It meant that anything you wanted to discard could be left in front of your house. If it hadn't been retrieved by scavengers by the collection date, the city's trucks would be by to gather it up and take it to the dump.

Finally, an opportunity to shop for the kids without needing cash, cards or coupons. From the outset of Junk Week, I would quietly pack the kids in the car and we'd cruise the neighbourhood streets for those items I had refused to buy but could find curbside. Seizing this opportunity to help ourselves, we picked up basketballs, mini trampolines, bikes and other discarded toys. While they shopped, I too would be on the look out for anything that might catch my eye.

In the early days, serious collection was a clandestine affair. Often in the middle of the night, you'd see the headlights of a pickup truck glaring at your own heap at the curb. The foragers would be wearing worm-picking caps to help them get a better look at the selection. Oftentimes your trash would be gone the next morning but a pile of new stuff replaced it.

For the casual shoppers like us, it was acceptable to do it in the daylight and each year more and more shoppers went public. One year a woman studying my old toaster oven yelled out to me, "Hey, this still work? Do you have the manual?" I remember thinking that I should have asked Joe's ex the same question before rescuing him from the curb. Please don't tell Joe I said that.

Each year we got more organized and excited about the possibilities that waited along the streets. One year my friend Lucia and I found a brand new mattress and box spring that was still sealed in plastic. Claiming it meant that she had to hang out the back window as I drove with my face pressed into the dashboard.

The year Lucia turned fifty I presented her with pieces I had scrounged from the streets of Oakville. Complete with chair, lamp, table and wall-art, all sprayed gold to commemorate this milestone birthday, there was enough stuff to furnish an entire room. It was really a shame she didn't have the four walls to contain it all.

In the midst of creating Lucia's 'room', I remembered seeing a gold leaf art deco clock in a pile of stuff at the end of the Bekkers' driveway. I had been perusing the mound while I was waiting for Alena to emerge from her piano lesson. I considered retrieving it at the time but thought that taking it might be tacky, since the Bekkers were our friends. Before I could make my final decision, Peter came out to chat. As we looked at his heap of junk, he commented that there had been a steady stream of customers and facetiously asked if I saw anything I liked. I lied.

"Are you kidding? I couldn't bring another thing home or I'd be tossed to the curb myself."

We left for home empty-handed.

But I couldn't stop thinking about that clock and soon convinced myself that I needed to have it to complete Lucia's golden décor. So the next morning as I headed off to tennis, I decided that when I was done, I would sneak back and scoop it from the Bekkers' heap of junk. I was bolstered by the knowledge that no one would be there to see me.

A few hours later I pulled up in front their house, left the car running, the door open, and ran over to the heap. With Lycra-clad butt up in the air, I started rummaging around to find the clock. Unable to locate it, I started moving things around. It was taking a lot longer than I thought it would. Where was it? Surely, it hadn't been claimed. Just as I went nose deep into the array of appliances, luggage and toys, I heard a voice.

"Heh. Is that who I think it is in there?"

Oh no. It was Peter. Wasn't he supposed to be at work? What was he doing home mid-afternoon?

"Aha! Caught you."

"Oh. Hi Peter," I said, blood rushing to my head as I remained face down in the junk heap.

"What the heck you doing in there?"

"Nothing."

"Right. Wait 'til this story gets around. Am I going to have fun with it."

I shuddered as he threw his head back and howled. After I extricated myself from the pile, I bemoaned the fact that I had been caught, but more importantly that I was leaving empty handed. Making matters worse, I knew that Peter would be true to his word, and that this would not be the end of it. And it wasn't.

Peter always acts as the bartender at our annual Christmas open house. Predictably, he used the junker story as an ice-breaker with every person he served that year. He and every-one else got a kick out of the animated way he mimicked my junk-retrieval technique, butt proudly saluting the ceiling.

Fair game, I guess. I just wish I had gotten that clock for Lucia's room.

A Child's Perspective

During a family trip to Italy in 1997, one of my favourite sights was in Positano on the Amalfi coast. Our view overlooked the spectacular cliffs and the deep magestic waters of the Tyrrhenian Sea.

One morning we decided to have breakfast at the home of our host, which was on a terraced area about a three hundred yard trek up from the water's edge. Sitting there, I could not believe the beauty of my surroundings. I was overcome by it all ... the view, the fresh smell of the sea, the colours and the sweet sounds around me of the family's pets: a dog, a goat and a parrot called Columbo.

Savouring the moment, and relishing the exquisite scenery, I leaned over to seven-year-old Alena and said, "Alena, isn't this awesome? Can you imagine what it would be like to live here?"

Alena smiled and nodded her head in agreement. "Oh, I know, Mommy ... to have a dog, a goat and a parrot ... it would be wonderful!"

Feeling the Nudge

*W*hen I was younger, I always remember my father directing his bony elbow into my side and nudging me. And in a harsh tone he'd say, "Now pay attention, you just might learn something!"

To be honest, I really wasn't interested in learning. But it did quiet me and forced me to try to listen. Even better, to watch what went on around me.

Since his death, I still feel the nudge from his spirit with the harshly whispered, "Pay attention ... to the pay attentions!"

It continues to fascinate me how a very long series of nudges, some gentle and some TKO's can set you along a path that meanders in ways you could never imagine.

In the winter of 2002, we made arrangements with our cousins to enjoy a weekend in southwest Massachusetts. The plan was to visit their son Ricky, who was spending a year at a prep school called Berkshire as a post graduate (meaning a year after graduating from high school) and watch one of his hockey games.

My arrival on campus that wintry day left an indelible mark on my mind with the vision of the school community beautifully nestled in and around the base of a mountain. I loved what I saw. The architecture was a blend of century old buildings, renovated structures and newly constructed facilities, all of which enhanced the sprawling campus. What a sight.

Everywhere we went that weekend caught my eye ... the arena adorned with crests from around the league, the dining hall with the array of flags from around the world and the casual and friendly atmosphere of everyone who strolled around the campus.

At one point, I remember standing in awe of my surroundings and announced to Joe, "Dante would love this place."

Joe, too, was enamored with what he saw. He wholeheartedly agreed.

At the time, Dante was in grade eleven and was part of what was referred to as the double cohort year. This meant that his graduating class would be the first group to finish high school after grade twelve rather than the traditional grade thirteen. Although many other provinces already were doing so, this was new to Ontario and we questioned his readiness for university before his eighteenth birthday.

Driving home that weekend the wheels started to turn about pursuing the 'prep school thing' for Dante. When we told him about it, the first thing he did was look it up on the computer. He liked what he saw. He was especially keen about the opportunity to participate in three sports. Football was his passion and he relished the idea of playing the American Game throughout New England. We, on the other hand were intrigued by the small class size, emphasis on academics and the mandatory two-hour study hall each night. We knew he would need all the academic prep that was offered if he wanted to realize his plan to go to university. When he had the chance to visit the campus that spring, it solidified his desire to attend Berkshire after graduation.

The next year, we started to put the plan into motion, sending transcripts, references, highlight tapes and fulfilling all of the mandatory requirements. Throughout the process we remained focused on the goal, but knew that it would be a long shot...not the acceptance part, but to obtain the necessary financial assistance to make it possible. It did not deter us from doing whatever we could to make it a reality.

In the spring of his graduating year, he received notice that his application had been accepted and that they were able to offer a small amount of financial aid to offset the high tuition (high by our standards as public school supporters). Regretably, we all knew it would not be feasible to accept the offer because it still required too much of a financial commitment from us. We had to decline. Joe and I were disappointed but Dante was devastated, as he had set his sights on the year away. We informed the school of our situation. In the meantime, Dante showed his resilience by making plans to go directly into university like most of his classmates.

However, three weeks later we received a call from Berkshire. They were now in a position to increase their offer. It was substantially more. But, in doing the calculations, it was still more money than we felt we could spend, considering that Joe had just retired and we still had the two other children to support. We discussed it privately.

Aside from the financial challenges, we had no experience with private school education, had never sent our kids away other than to summer camp and our relationship with the U.S. was limited to cross border shopping and the occasional visit to Joe's family in San Francisco. Now crunch time, we were getting nervous about making the decision. They gave us twenty-four hours to think about it.

It consumed us. Together we had to agree on our support before we presented it to Dante for a decision. As I sat at my desk, with it all swirling around in my head, I closed my eyes and sent a message to my dad. Peo, please send me a sign that this is something we should do.

That day, a new family moved in next door. When Alena came home from school, she excitedly announced, "Mom, I met our new neighbour. She's in my class and she has a brother who's fifteen. She said he goes to a school in the states."

"Really. Whereabouts?"

"I don't know but I think it's a prep school."

Hmmm. That was interesting because until our visit to Berkshire I hadn't known anything about prep schools and to that point, my cousin's son Ricky was the only person I knew who attended one.

As I sat, still mulling it over, someone came to the front door. It was our new neighbour in need of a Band-Aid. As I obliged, I asked the woman about her family. She proceeded to inform me about each of the children. She then mentioned that one of the boys went to school in Massachusetts.

"Massachusetts? Really. What school?"

"Oh, it's a prep school. It's called Berkshire."

There were no bells, no whistles, no clanging of pots or bolts of lightening. But there was a nudge so sharp I felt the pain and reached for my side. My father had answered my call. There are over seventy-five prep schools in the eastern states. There are only three hundred and seventy-five students at Berkshire, and they hail from over seventeen countries. What were the chances our next-door neighbour would be one of them?

I looked up. I said thank you to my dad and quickly went to the kitchen to share this with Joe.

An hour later, we sat down with Dante and asked him if he would still like to go to Berkshire, given the new circumstances. He had until ten the next morning to decide. By five minutes past ten, I was on the phone accepting their offer.

That was April 2003. We have just closed the book on our final chapter with Berkshire. Dante graduated from there in 2004, Vincent in 2006 and Alena most recently in 2009.

More than our passports bear the markings of that segment of time. It proved to be a life enhancing experience for all of us, which included frequent travel, numerous athletic competitions and many meaningful relationships. Each of us will treasure our brush with Berkshire. We remain eternally grateful for having the opportunity to be welcomed into their community. We remain equally appreciative of having felt the nudge and paying attention. It was worth it.

Cruising Out of Control

When I was in university one of my career goals was to be a recreation director on a cruise ship. It never happened, but I have been on two cruises and participated in activities organized by the fun squads. Witnessing their antics from the sidelines, I invariably find myself shaking my head in awe, marveling at their seemingly limitless energy and their effortless ways of getting people involved. I enjoy watching them, knowing that when I was their age I, too, would have been equipped to handle all that this grueling career demanded. And it sure would have been fun.

A few years ago Joe and I joined a group of friends on a March Break cruise. One night after dinner, all the women in our group enthusiastically decided to dance our way from bar to bar, and while we started out as an eager crowd, by eleven o'clock there were just two of us left, Maryann and me. Pooped from the partying, we flopped down and kicked off our shoes in the final nightclub of the evening. We were done. Sitting there exhausted, we enjoyed one final drink and waited for the scheduled show to begin. We were satisfied with our front row seats and wished that we could beckon the rest of our group to join us, but neither one of us wanted to move. We settled in, listening to the taped music and watching the staff prepare for the show.

Out of nowhere, a few members of the club's entertainment staff suddenly appeared in front of us and one began pulling insistently on my arm to join them. Oh no, why me? I must have some kind of neon sign on my head that periodically flashes the message, 'Pick me, Pick me', because this was by no means the first time that I had unwittingly been singled out. With Maryann laughing and encouraging them to continue their efforts (it took the pressure off her), they managed to pull me along the floor to a secret room hidden away behind some large plants. I didn't have a clue what I was in for, nor was I keen to find out.

Once backstage, I saw that six of us had been kidnapped. They informed us that we would comprise a significant part of the show (Please, God, not that hypnotism thing again). The theme was *Grease* and we would be required to dress in character and then called upon to be part of a dance contest. Maybe, I thought, it's not a neon sign after all, but a magnet buried beneath my skin that pulls them irresistibly to me. Anyway, at the mere mention of a costume I started to panic, recalling numerous ill-fitting selections from my past. And I was right. Nothing they had in the ladies' costume cupboard was close to my size, although the guys' stuff would have fit for sure.

There I stood looking hideous in a wig, cropped blouse and skirt that would not do up. Since there were no size eleven and a half shoes for my dainty feet, I opted to go barefoot. Out we paraded to the dance floor to face what had by then become a large crowd (I guess they had studied their event schedule). I was thankful that we had decided not to call the others in our group. Making a fool of yourself in front of strangers is one thing, in front of your friends quite another.

The contest required us to compete as three couples, culminating in a dance-off. The show began with an instructor teaching us the moves and steps; the practice of the routine followed; then each couple's performance was judged by the crowd.

My partner was at best four inches shorter than me and a good twenty-five pounds lighter. His makeup was thick; he had sunglasses on and a hat so it was impossible to tell what he really looked like. And me, well who knows what kind of apparition I resembled but I assumed it was probably something like Tootsie in drag.

One of the moves required my partner to hoist me to his hips followed by a slide between his legs and a two handed lift back to the upright position. I apologized to him in advance.

It was definitely one of those situations that required me to give a pep talk ... to myself. After all, since I was stuck there I might as well make the best of it. Besides, no one in the audience would recognize me anyway, and hopefully they had all been drinking. I just wished I had too.

The competition started and I called upon Lucille Ball's spirit to help me have some fun with this. We hammed it up, we improvised and I did my best not to lead as I had been trained to do in the all-girl gym classes of my youth. When it came time for the lifts, the poor guy nearly broke his back so we called out for some assistance to carry it (and me) off.

The entire contest segment lasted about twenty minutes. Mortified, panting and dreadfully embarrassed, I made my way back to Maryann after the show. She was still trying to regain consciousness after nearly choking herself over the hilarity of my performance. Oh, how she wished the others could have been there and oh, how thankful I was that they were not.

At breakfast the next morning, Maryann did her best to recount every single moment of the show for them so I could live my mortification anew. Adding to my pleasure, some fellow travelers came over to acknowledge my efforts of the previous night. I was surprised that they recognized me ... so much for my speculation about drinking and recognition.

As we waited to board the ship after an excursion a few days later, a man of smaller stature tapped me on the shoulder and said, "Thank you very much for the other night."

Oh dear. Which night? Had I had too much to drink? Did I do something I should regret? What exactly was he referring to?

My face must have been registering the question ... 'and what might you be thanking me for?' because he quickly reminded me that he had been my partner in the contest at the nightclub. Surprised, I hugged him and apologized repeatedly over his shoulder. He assured me that it had been the most fun he had ever had, especially since he was not one to brave anything like that in front of others. We laughed about it and I added, "Well, at least it wasn't caught on tape."

How wrong I was.

"Oh, it's definitely on tape. Not only did they film us, but it's on all the ship's monitors and cabin TVs. It's part of the loop that's on every hour for the rest of the week."

I grimaced. He continued excitedly:

"Actually, the tape's available for purchase. Oh, and if you're interested, there are plenty of photos on display on the second floor for all your friends to see."

Great. Next time I'm faking an injury.

Finding the Joy in Yoga

This past year as I set off for my annual volunteer adventure, I didn't know what to expect because I left all of the planning up to my new internet friend John-Arthur Miller. From his office at the Sheffield Senior Center, he searched out the services I might work with, made all the contacts and ultimately prepared my schedule for the week. And he did it all willingly and with endless enthusiasm.

Arriving in Sheffield, Massachusetts, I quickly got comfortable at the nearby bed and breakfast, The Staveleigh House, where I became immediate friends with Ali Winston, the innkeeper. She and her hospitality provided the soft landing for me at the end of each day of service.

The activities John Arthur arranged for me were quite varied. It was apparent that no matter where I was sent, there was always a component of it to enjoy. And in most cases, it was meeting the people. Everyone was warm and welcoming to me as a visitor to their small community.

My fully scheduled week of services from morning to night took me to the likes of senior centres, the food bank, the local library, a kindergarten class, group homes and more. It was eventful, with every visit opening the door to yet another view of the Sheffield-Great Barrington area and the wonderful people who claim it as their home.

On my final day I visited a farmhouse outside of town,

where a small group of adults with special needs lived. It was there that I met a young woman, Natasha, and her volunteer assistant, John, with whom I would be spending the morning. After a short visit at the home, I took my spot in the backseat to accompany them to their morning activities and assist in whatever way was necessary.

En route, they were both keen to give me all the background information they felt I needed about their routine and the range of services available to them in the community. We dropped by CATA (Community Access to the Arts) where visual and performing arts opportunities are provided for adults with physical/developmental disabilities. I was impressed. Natasha had a full schedule of non-stop fun and learning, not to mention a caring and comfortable home where she could live independently, yet be surrounded by the love and watchful eyes of the others.

We finally headed to our morning destination, the Berkshire South Regional Community Center, where they told me we would be taking some classes. In the parking lot, there was a buzz in the air as cars, vans and mini buses unloaded the group of participants. One by one, they filed out of their vehicles, some walking on their own and others accompanied by a helper. Although their ages, sizes and disabilities varied, they shared one similarity ... they were all excited to be there. I was anxious to fall in line behind them, not wanting to miss out. So I followed.

Entering the centre, each one offered a personal greeting to the staff, ranging from bear hugs to animated waves. Any paperwork or phone talk ceased as the noise level increased and their energy flooded the area. The group settled in front of the large gymnasium. As everyone shimmied and shuffled around in preparation for their class, I asked John and Natasha what was scheduled. They told me that we would be there for two classes, juggling and yoga. I expressed concern about my clothing. They both assured me I would be fine.

Instead of juggling that morning, we had Michael, who led

our class of twenty adults with special needs and fifteen helpers in a session of paper airplane flying. He patiently taught us how to fold the paper, tweak it and ultimately fly it. The group's enthusiasm was contagious and over the course of the hour we repeatedly released our planes amidst great appreciation and applause.

Without us realizing it, Michael continued to challenge us and our airplane flinging skills. Before the class was over, he managed to coach most of us to send our airplanes soaring through a series of suspended hoola hoops. There was lots of excitement over the trials, failures and ultimately the success of them flying through the hoops. The Olympics had nothing on the jubilation that filled the room when a plane successfully floated through the course. Wow, it was exhilarating. I was ready for lunch, but was reminded that we still had another class. Yoga. Oh no. I am not a fan of yoga.

We all stayed in the gym. Michael gathered up his props and left to a round of applause as Paula, the yoga instructor took her place in the middle of the room. She was all of five-foot-not-much but her smile magnified her. As we jockeyed for position on the floor with our mats, Paula went around and greeted everyone by name. When I looked around I did not see anyone wearing any of the customary specialized yoga wear that I was used to seeing: no high performance clothing, no special fabrics with breathability, no logos or colour-coordinated outfits at all. They wore ski pants, corduroys, blue jeans and heavy sweats. Everyone looked comfortable and judging by their smiles, they appeared happy to be there.

As Paula looked out at us waiting in our chosen spots on the floor, she joyfully invited us to sit on our mats to begin the first exercise.

"I want you to stretch your legs forward. As you straighten your legs, point your toes and lean back as far as you can. Reach behind you with your hands and look at the ceiling."

Her voice was calm yet commanding. Her instructions were slow but thorough, making certain we all understood. She never stopped moving as she quietly moved around the room to offer assistance. As I positioned myself according to her direction, I suddenly saw a pair of arms headed my way. The young man in front was slowly sliding into his own position, when he reached back and felt my feet. He did not stop. He proceeded to reach back further, grip my ankles and begin a gentle foot massage on my size eleven and a halfs. His helper turned to me and mouthed the words, "He loves feet. Is that okay with you?"

I assured her that it was more than okay as I moved my feet closer to his touch.

Paula continued to effortlessly encourage us to follow her movements. As she did, you could hear talking, rustling and other bodily sounds. No one blinked, budged or was bothered by it. I was getting a kick out of this. But it wasn't until Paula led us into the downward dog position that the gates of levity opened. When she announced that it was time for 'that dog position', the calamity began. Everyone had something to say.

"Paula, I have a dog. Do you have a dog?"

"Yes I do."

"What's your dog's name, Paula? My dog's name is Buttercup."

"Buttercup? That's a funny name."

"I have cat. He's really old though."

"Meow, meow. That's what a cat sounds like."

"My mother has a bird."

And the banter continued from one participant to another. They all freely commented, some laughing, others barking and me shaking my head with pleasure.

Paula did not frown upon them nor did she utter a plea to put an end to it. She kept the movement going, showing patience for all of us. Smiling and keeping her composure, she continued to lead us through her class. I later learned that she is a trained dancer and a student of improv, both invaluable skills for her role as yoga instructor.

Paula ended our class that morning looking out at each of us with a beautiful smile. She clasped her hands together and recited, "Namaste ... may the divinity be with you."

I truly believe it was. I felt the joy in that yoga class. I thanked Paula for sharing her enthusiasm and energy with us, and told her that she had renewed my faith in the discipline. I even suggested her class be mandatory for all yoga instructors.

A few days later, as I was packing up at the end of my volunteer adventure, I reviewed the events of my week. I thought about the parts I would treasure most. The yoga class was number one.

Who Said No One Watches Cable?

I am a stickler for fairness ... fairness with customers, with students, with athletes. I will be the first one with something to say when an injustice has occurred. I have been threatened with ejection at a basketball game after merely suggesting they check the sheet to correct the score. I have been known to propel a retail complaint directly to the president. And yes, I have on occasion contributed my two cents worth to opposing coaches when I have witnessed unfair treatment on their part. When I encounter this type of situation, it's best to prepare myself in advance for a more gentle approach.

But often there just isn't time. Because when the Taurean side of my nature exposes its riled head in fury, there's no interfering with my pursuit.

One such occurrence took place at Nelson Stadium in Burlington on a cold, damp and miserable Saturday in November. It was BMFA (Burlington Minor Football Association) Championship Day 1993. Coincidentally, the remaining two teams in the Tyke final involved both my son Dante and nephew Andrew. Dante, eight, played a limited role on The Ironmen team, while eleven year old Andrew was one of the stars of the undefeated Volunteers.

It was obvious to everyone that the Volunteers were destined to maintain their flawless record with yet another win to cap off the season. After all, they were the bigger, better, stronger, faster and more aggressively coached team. The underdog Ironmen, on the other hand, knew it would be a challenge for them and secretly as parents, we just prayed for our little boys to finish the game without injuries. But that predetermined conclusion did not prevent us from cheering our hearts out for them, yelling encouraging words like:

"C'mon boys you can do it!."

"One play at a time.!"

"Nice run!."

"Good block.!"

"Keep trying. Hang in there!"

"We love you. You're winners to us!"

Huddled together in our section of the stands, we rallied in support of our team. In the adjacent section, the parents in orange did their best to support their boys as well, while respecting both the difference in skill level and the win-loss record of each team. Their coach however had a different agenda.

From the outset, the Volunteers had control of the field, weaving in, out and around the Ironmen. It seemed they could score at will. 7 - 0. 14 - 0. 21 - 0. 28 - 0. With each score, we shouted more encouragement to our boys and as we did, the opposing parents respectfully said less. Although they became more subdued, their coach seemed to relish every score with smug glances at the opposing bench and glares to us in the stands. Before the half, they scored yet one more time to make it 35 - 0 and as they did, the coach turned to look up at our clump of green and gold, pointed aggressively in our direction and shouted, "Take that."

I was shocked by his behavior and furious with his remark. Without hesitation or preparation, having lost all sense of decorum and control, I bolted up from my seat in the stands, releasing myself from the tucked in blankets around me. With my loudest 'outdoor' voice, I shouted back "Where do you get off yelling out to us like that? What do you mean by *take that?* Do you think this is fun for our boys? Do you not have any sense of decency? Do you not understand the meaning of recreation? These are young boys here and there you are Mr. Hotshot coach rubbing it in our faces. Why are you trying to embarrass them? Are you pissed off at us for some reason?"

As I ranted, Joe tugged at my side to sit down. I had created a scene in response to his unprovoked attack on us. He finally managed to pull me back into my seat. It took a few minutes for my breathing to settle. Parents close by reached over, back and across to offer their thanks for defending them and the boys. When I seemed to have regained control, Joe leaned over and whispered, "Honey, the Cogeco Community TV crew is here. They caught it all on tape."

Judging by the calls I received every blessed time they played the tape, there is one thing for certain ... there is a HUGE audience for Cable TV.

I debated whether I should call Cogeco to purchase the Master Tape. Dante debated inviting me to any more of his games.

Painful But Memorable

$\mathcal{V}$ery early in my young career as a wisecracker, a clown, a smart ass, a joker, a tease, a card or any other name that one with a quick tongue and a strong sense of humour might be referred to, my idea of fun was often frowned upon. Experiencing this only served to thicken my skin and toughen my spirit.

Grade three. Holy Rosary School in Thorold. My teacher was a very stern Sister Mary Something. For most of that year, I kept my place: last seat, row three, just in front of the cloakroom. There I wondered my days away, staring at the boys' sneakers (oh, how I craved a pair of P.F. Flyers) and trying desperately to solve yet another one of life's great mysteries.

In grade three, at the age of eight, our unsolved mystery question of the year was: do nuns have hair? We'd talk about it at recess; we'd chat while waiting to skip double dutch; we'd discuss it as we walked home for lunch; and we'd wallow in it all weekend long. You see, if it was true that at any time, any one of us could get The Call … that is, to be swayed to become a nun, I had to know the answer to this very important question. After all, it was one of only four possible career choices for young women at the time, the others being teacher, nurse or secretary. The hair issue was an important factor in this choice.

Time passed and grade three was proving to be quite uneventful, unless you counted the regular 'turtle drills' that we commonly practiced in preparation for a nuclear blast. Yes, once a week at the sound of the air raid siren screaming from the top of Whyte Avenue, right next to the giant water cooler in the sky, we would be ordered to quickly line up and parade through the school. We'd shuffle along in one long uniformed line until we reached the hallowed halls of downstairs. At Sister's command, we'd drop to our knees, hunch over and clasp our hands together behind our head. Stifled snickers, anonymous body noises and uncontrollable laughter would follow until we got the signal to stand up and parade back to our class, safe from the threat of attack once more.

Well, I don't quite know how it happened, but one day I found myself at the head of the line directly behind the teacher. Quite odd, considering I was the tallest in the class, a distinction that had earned me the perpetual position of power ... last.

I nervously accepted my new position and waited for her signal. Sister swung around. It was seconds before her flowing habit fell into place. Pausing momentarily for the line to settle, she then began the march, leading the way in her black oxfords. Cued by the push from behind I knew it was time to proceed. Up the stairs we climbed. I used all of my weight to hold the others back as they continued to push forward.

My eyes never left the long black veil trailing down her back to the floor, for fear that I might inadvertently touch it. I guess it had a hypnotic effect on me because before I could say 'Amen' I had obviously taken one step too many. I had underestimated the length of my stride and the vastness of her veil. All I remember was the look she wore as her head darted around to grasp whatever was left of the flowing fabric as it pulled away from her head ... from beneath my shoe.

As she scowled I froze, and the herd behind dominoed into my back. We all lunged forward; our eyes bulged in horror at the sight. The whispers rushed in a wave that slowly crawled up the stairs behind me. "She's got hair, she's got hair, she's got hair."

Mouth stretched open and eyes inflated, I couldn't believe what I had done. I knew this was the worst thing to happen to me since the first confession incident, when I used my outdoor voice in the confession for all my classmates to hear.

In silent anguish I mouthed the words, "I'm sorry," to Sister, but her eyes were too glazed over to notice. Upon arriving at the classroom, I remember lowering my head and quickly retreating to my sacred spot at the back of the room. Once back in my seat, I said a prayer so that Sister would not hate me forever and silently pleaded, Please, Dear Jesus, don't let her hold a grudge.

For the next few days I sat quietly. I passed no notes. I did not once lift my knees and walk around the room in my desk. I even held back from letting any funny comments float up to the front of the class to see who might laugh. No, there was none of that. I was on my very best behaviour, hoping that Sister's memory would fade in time. Which seemed to work, until about three days later.

It was time for Social Studies. Sister asked the girl in the first seat of the first row to begin reading from the text as we all followed along. Out loud she read, "And then the Native Indian went to sleep in his tip-pee."

Well, I heard the mispronounced word and I couldn't hold back my laughter. My Auntie Mary's dog was named Tippy and I thought that was pretty funny. I let out a few loud snorts, expecting my classmates to follow suit. They didn't.

It's never a good sign when you're the only one laughing. I saw my friends staring back at me like I had three heads, but unaffected by their looks and not wanting to spoil my pleasure, I lifted the lid of my desk so that I could laugh quietly inside it. But it only made things worse because it served as an echo chamber. As I tried to catch my breath and regain composure, I heard the shuffling of cloth and the rattling of beads, interrupted only by the pounding of a pair of size four oxfords. Oh, no! She hadn't forgotten.

Next thing I knew, I was yanked up by my white cotton blouse and dragged to the front of the class. As I stood there facing my classmates, they seemed as worried for me as I was for myself. Sister opened her top drawer and took out the eighteen-inch leather strap that was kept for the gravest infractions. Standing slightly taller already than Sister herself, I looked out at my classmates. I silently assured myself: They're on my side. They know I mean well. I make them laugh. I'm the best home run hitter on their team.

They stared back at me, clearly hoping that it would never ever happen to them, and anxious for the bell to ring so they could run and find my sister to tell on me. Biting my lip and trying really hard not to cry in anticipation of both the embarrassment and pain, I proceeded to get the strap. What I got was one very high and hard flick of the hunk of leather on top my outstretched hand. My hand stung from the slap and my heart hurt from the humiliation. To save face I turned to Sister and said, "Thank you very much, Sister. I really enjoyed that."

I swallowed the lump, held back my tears and returned to my seat as my friends gawked at me in sympathy.

My sister Sharon, who was at another school in the neighbourhood, got the report before I arrived home for lunch. I begged her not to tell on me because we both knew what it would mean. It was certain that I would get the strap once again … at home. So she kept me in check from that point on by merely motioning strap to hand whenever there was something she wanted from me. It worked. I would do just about anything to prevent her from spilling it to my parents.

I'm embarrassed to admit that it wasn't until I was sixteen years old that I finally answered her back with, "Who cares? Tell them."

My poor mother could only look at me and shake her head as though to say, "It figures." With everything else I was dishing out as a teenager, apparently this incident from ancient history didn't merit much of her attention. And although the days of the strap were long gone, I was nonetheless relieved to escape her belated reproof ... and ecstatic (in an immature, grade three kind of way), that Sharon finally had to relinquish her title of Sister of Perpetual Power.

P.S. So, I guess that day in grade three was when it all began, me seeing humour in the simple things ... the simple things that are so often overlooked or unrecognized by others. Since then I have learned that even though I may often have to laugh alone and perhaps even suffer consequences, I will continue to look for, uncover and share the humour that is everywhere.

~!!~

About Carole

Carole Bertuzzi Luciani is a professional speaker who has spoken to hundreds of thousands of individuals since 1980. As a self-proclaimed 'Moodivator', she both enlightens and entertains the audiences she reaches throughout North America.

Her topics are diverse and include: 'Achieve Balance - Recycle Yourself for the Future', 'Dealing with the Public', 'Humour ... Sure Beats Stress' and 'Be Moodivated'. Each is delivered in an engaging manner and sprinkled with her unique brand of humour. Audiences cannot help but 'get the message'.

Carole successfully blends the demands of her work with the pleasures of her play and is proud to admit they often overlap.

Whether your group is large or intimate in size; a paid booking; or a community service commitment, Carole strives toward the same goal ... that you leave feeling better than you did when you arrived.

Check out Carole's websites for more information and how you may have an opportunity to hear one of the popular CBL Presentations.

www.carolebertuzziluciani.com (Personal)

www.moodivator.ca (CBL Presentations Inc.)